The New Forest landscape

A report prepared by
Land Use Consultants
for the
Countryside Commission

Published by:
Countryside Commission
John Dower House
Crescent Place
Cheltenham, Glos GL50 3RA
Tel: 0242 521381
© Countryside Commission 1986

Distributed by:
Countryside Commission
Publications Despatch Department
19/23 Albert Road
Manchester M19 2EQ
CCP 220
Price £5.00 including postage

Acknowledgements

Particular thanks are due to David Stagg for his generous assistance and advice and for allowing access to his library. We are also grateful for the assistance of Colin Tubbs of the Nature Conservancy Council, Nicholas Bannister and Roy Hughes of the Forestry Commission, Vernon Hazel of Hampshire County Council, Alan Foster of New Forest District Council, Anthony Pasmore, June Irvine and John Lavender.

Figures 2, 3 and 4 are based on information from the Ordnance Survey 1:25,000 map of the New Forest, on the Forestry Commission's Compartment Stock Maps, on the Nature Conservancy Council's vegetation maps, and on maps in Colin Tubbs' book *An Ecological History of the New Forest*.

Photographs by Ianthe Ruthven, Edward Holdaway and R. K. Knightbridge.

British Library Cataloguing in Publication Data

The New Forest landscape: a report.
1. Landscape —— England —— New Forest
I. Land Use Consultants II. Great Britain.
Countryside Commission
719'.0-9422'75   QH77.G7

ISBN 0-86170-187-9

Designed and produced by CGS Studios – Cheltenham
Printed by Cotswold Printing Company – Stroud

Contents

Figures

Foreword

The Countryside Commission has long held the view that the New Forest is of equivalent quality to a national park for the natural beauty and amenity of its landscape and the opportunities it affords for open-air recreation.

Our purpose in publishing this report is to set down in some detail the special qualities of the landscape, which many people agree is of national, if not international, significance. It does not reproduce the numerous statements on the nature conservation interest of the Forest, nor examine recreation except where it interacts with landscape. Rather it tries to complement these statements by highlighting the many facets of the New Forest landscape which have enthralled people for centuries.

We were considerably heartened by the favourable response which this report received in draft form, and we are most grateful for the time given by those who commented. All suggestions were considered seriously and most have led to amendments. We hope that the statement will now be of use to all organisations when judging the landscape consequences of policies and proposals which might affect the New Forest.

The consultations also revealed two particular points of concern. The first was that the report did not produce a landscape management plan and did not contain a clear statement of the Commission's views on detailed issues such as drainage and vegetation management. The second was the question of whether or not the Forest should be designated a national park.

It was never the intention of the report to take the form of a management plan for the landscape. Our aim was to identify the key elements of the landscape and the factors that have shaped it in the past and are affecting it now. A management plan could not have been prepared in isolation from other aspects of the Forest, nor without the involvement of numerous organisations. The most appropriate place for the Commission to express its views on management issues is in the Open Forest Committee and other consultation arrangements set up by the Forestry Commission. With the publication of this report future discussions on management issues in the Forest will be based on a better understanding of the unique landscape asset which it represents.

The question of national park status for the Forest has been the subject of debate on many occasions, both within the Commission and outside. We draw a distinction between

- the national importance of the Forest for landscape and recreation.
- the most appropriate statutory mechanism for recognising that importance and ensuring appropriate management.

On the former, we believe the New Forest to be of equivalent quality to a national park. But the normal statutory mechanism — a national park authority set up under the National Parks and Access to the Countryside Act 1949 — is not the most appropriate for the New Forest. No other national park is dominated by Crown land managed by a Government agency over which common rights are administered by verderers set up by statute.

The Commission's immediate aim is to ensure through existing measures that landscape conservation and appropriate provision for recreation are pursued in the New Forest with the same vigour as in the national parks. This requires recognition of the New Forest's status as equivalent to a national park, not only in protection from inappropriate development, but in terms of the way it is managed and the resources made available to it.

Sir Derek Barber
Chairman
Countryside Commission

1. On Forest scenery

In the late 1700's, the Vicar of Boldre in the southern part of the New Forest in Hampshire set out on a journey through the Forest and its surroundings. Nervously noting the lack of a turnpike road to guide him, the variety of paths which might mislead, and the presence of large bogs (which he considered to be 'deceitful ground' in which the unwary traveller may flounder) he felt obliged to take to horseback, and to seek the services of one of the under-keepers of the forest as a guide. On his journey he called on a number of the local gentry in their great houses, visiting the likes of Sir John D'Oyly, the Duke of Bolton, Lord Delaware and Lord Bute among others. He admired their property, calling Lord Bute's house "a sumptuous pile" but at the end of his travels he returned to his own more modest parsonage house at Vicar's Hill where he could admire the sun setting over the Forest at the end of the day.

What are we to make of this journey? Simply an eighteenth century country parson making the rounds of a parish which happened to be populated by particularly wealthy parishioners? Far from it, for during his residence at Boldre the Vicar had cause to devote himself to the relief of the material and spiritual poverty of his parishioners who were mainly "cottagers of the poorest description . . . who were exposed to every temptation of pillage and robbery from their proximity to the deer, the game and the fuel of the forest". No, this journey, one of many made in the New Forest beween his arriving in Boldre in 1777 and his death in 1804, had another quite different purpose. For this particular Vicar of Boldre was the Reverend William Gilpin, champion of the cause of "picturesque beauty". His journeys in the New Forest were certainly not concerned with the spiritual well-being of his parishioners for, as he himself wrote: "we are in quest only of scenery".

Before arriving in Boldre Gilpin had made several tours of the most scenic areas of Britain, visiting the Wye Valley, parts of South Wales, the Lake District and the Highlands of Scotland. He published his writings on these tours while at Boldre, and in them proposed "a new object of pursuit, that of examining the face of a country by the rules of picturesque beauty". When he became the Vicar of Boldre, Gilpin says of the New Forest that he had:

"little intention of wandering farther among its fences, than the bounds of my own Parish, or of amusing myself anymore with writing on picturesque subjects. But one scene drew me on to another; till at length I had traversed the whole forest. I had been much among lakes and mountains: but I had never lived in a forest. I knew little of its scenery. Everything caught my attention . . . I made minutes of what I observed . . . Thus, as small things lead to greater, an evening walk, or ride, became the foundation of a volume"

The volume to which he refers - or more correctly three volumes - is his work *Remarks on Forest Scenery and other woodland views, relative chiefly to picturesque beauty, illustrated by the scenery of the New Forest, Hampshire* published in 1791. In it he dwells at great length on the picturesque quality of trees and forests in general and of the New Forest in particular. It says much for the quality of the New Forest landscape that Gilpin considered it to be equally worthy of his consideration as the landscapes of the Lake District and the Scottish Highlands. But in beginning his description of the New Forest Gilpin is sweeping in his praise:

"Within equal limits perhaps few parts of England afford a greater variety of beautiful landscape. Its woody scenes, its extended lawns, and vast sweeps of wild country, unlimited by artificial boundaries, together with its river views and distant coasts; are all in a great degree magnificent."

The Cattle Ford, Liney Hill Wood.

Walter Crane illustration from J R Wise, The New Forest, 1895 edition.

The word forest immediately suggests the idea of a continued uninterrupted tract of woody country. But forests in general are much more varied. They consist indeed of tracts of woody country. But these tracts are, at the same time intermixed with patches of pasturage, which commonly bear the same proportion to the woods of the forest, which lawns do to the clumps of a park.

Rev W Gilpin, *Remarks on Forest Scenery,* 1791.

The Forest today is a mosaic of old woodland, of managed forestry Inclosures, of extensive tracts of heathland, grassy lawns and of enclosed areas of farmland and villages.

Gilpin's appreciation of the New Forest landscape influenced the thinking and writing of many who came after him. Nearly one hundred years later, in 1875, when the wholesale destruction of the ancient woodlands and enclosure of open land had led to a special inquiry by a House of Commons Select Committee, we find Henry Fawcett, Professor of Political Economy at Cambridge University giving evidence about the New Forest in terms which sound remarkably similar to Gilpin's introductory remarks.

"It is an open space perfectly unequalled in its character; it possesses a beauty which certainly no other open space in the kingdom, known to me, possesses; . . . there are scattered trees grouped in the most beautiful way, and they derive a great part of their beauty from the open glades and wide stretches of heath, with which they are interspersed."

Similar remarks about the unique qualities of the landscape occur in much of the subsequent writing about the New Forest.

But in its wild scenery lies its greatest charm. From every hill-top gleam the blue waters of the English Channel, broken in the foreground by the long line of the Isle of Wight downs and the white chalk walls of the Needles. Nowhere, in extent at least, spread such stretches of heath and moor, golden in the spring with the blaze of furze, and in the autumn purple with heather, and bronzed with the fading fern. Nowhere in England rise such oak-woods, their boughs rimed with the frostwork of lichens, and dark beech-groves with their floor of red brown leaves, on which the branches weave their own warp and the woof of light and shade.

J R Wise, *The New Forest : Its History and Scenery*, First Edition, 1863.

2. The New Forest landscape today

While descriptions of the picturesque qualities of the landscape were accepted as a proper form of study in the late eighteenth and nineteenth centuries, today the emphasis has changed. Many people are now able to travel quite widely and experience landscape for themselves. There is, therefore, less need for a privileged few to pass on what they have seen, for others to enjoy at secondhand. The development of photography and television has also contributed to the demise of landscape appreciation. Good photographs or films can evoke the character of a landscape in a way which can make the written word seem largely redundant. We have also increasingly come to take landscapes for granted and not to give specific thought to exactly why some of them are so special. Growth in concern for the environment in general, and ecology in particular, and the rise of recreation as a force in the countryside have also meant that specialist writing has increasingly focussed on ecological matters or on the modern pressures for recreation.

These changes have influenced the New Forest as much as other areas. But though the fashion for description of scenery may have passed, the landscape of the New Forest which so inspired Gilpin still remains. It is not of course unchanged and many of the scenes which Gilpin describes have been much altered over the years. But the essence of the picturesque quality which he, and others after him, described in such detail is still clearly apparent and the individual elements which contribute to this beauty, still remain. Before turning to a more detailed examination of exactly what it is that constitutes the landscape of the New Forest today, let us attempt first of all to evoke something of its special qualities. These are the characteristics which cannot fail to strike anyone who visits it or lives in or near it.

A stranger to the New Forest would be struck most forcibly by the fact that it is not really a 'forest' at all, in today's common usage of the word. It is by no means all wooded country, although there are extensive woodlands within it. Rather it is a mosaic of old woodland, of managed forestry Inclosures, of extensive tracts of heathland with boggy ground in the lower lying parts, of grassy lawns and of enclosed areas of farmland and villages. It is possible within a short distance to move from the dappled shade and towering branches of ancient beech woods to the high, windswept heathland of the northern ridges, where there is a sense of space and freedom more often associated with areas such as Dartmoor, Exmoor or the North York Moors. It is these contrasts, and the varied nature of the edges formed between open land and woodland, which are so essential to the character of the New Forest. Each part acts as a foil to the other; from within the shelter and security of a woodland there are tantalising views over the open spaces beyond; from the exposed open spaces there are nearly always receding vistas of wooded skylines formed by the billowing crowns of the deciduous woodlands, or the dark regular outlines of the conifer plantations or perhaps a mixture of the two.

Although much reduced in extent since Gilpin's day, the unenclosed woods of the Forest, widely known as the Ancient and Ornamental Woodlands, retain a sense of great beauty and tranquillity as well as embodying the long history of Forest use and management. There are trees of many different ages, with some of the great pollarded trees dating from the 1600s still providing an awe inspiring presence. The beauty of these woods lies not only in these large old trees, but in the natural form of the woodland; the random spacing of trees of different ages; in the presence in many parts of a dark contrasting understorey of holly; in the opening of the woodland to form grassy glades; in the presence of the small, slow moving meandering streams and still pools; and in the everchanging patterns of light and shade on leaves, bark and grass. These woods remain the epitome of Gilpin's sylvan landscape and, to many, lie at the heart of the beauty and mystery of the New Forest.

Stepping out from the shade and enclosure of the woodlands, the scene is quite different. Large expanses of open heathland or grass lawn stretch away into the distance offering an opportunity, rare in lowland England, for unhindered access on foot and freedom to wander in open country. This is the part of the Forest where the plateaus provide a sense of height, of open prospect and of exposure to the elements which is much greater than one would expect from the actual elevation of the country, and where the lower lying 'bottoms' are often secret and sheltered. There are high points and outlooks where the wide expanses of heathland can be seen rolling away in waves like a vast sea and where sunrise and sunset bring subtle creeping changes in colour to the expanses of heather, bracken and gorse.

But it is not only at the beginning and end of the day that colour plays such an important part in the landscape of the Forest. The woods and the heaths together form an ever-changing palette of colours which alters with the season and with the weather. In winter the tones are sombre. The brown and dun of the heather is set alongside the dark heavy green, sometimes almost black, shades of the gorse and the scattered clumps or specimens of Scots pine, with both offset by the russet tones of the dormant bracken, and the cream swathes of the winter foliage of moor grass. In spring there are the sharp bright greens of new growth - the shooting bracken, the new leaves bursting on the oak and beech trees, the fresh growth of grass on the lawns. In summer all is heavy and green, with the dark hues of the heathland punctuated by the bright yellow flowering of the gorse, and the first purple haze of the heather flowers. In autumn the woodlands display all the splendour of the turning leaves in shades of gold and red and yellow, thick carpets of rustling leaves form under the canopy and beyond, on the open heath, the heather still blooms in a sea of purple.

. . . it is not a forest in the ordinary sense of the word. There are scattered trees grouped in the most beautiful way, and they derive a great part of their beauty from the open glades and wide stretches of heath, with which they are interspersed. Nothing can be more unlike the New Forest than close and dense woods.

Henry Fawcett, in Evidence to 1875 Select Committee.

One of the great characteristics of the New Forest as compared with other forests, is that there is less wooded than openland; it is an open forest, it is not wood; it never was intended by nature to be a continuous wood; if you make it a continuous wood, it is no longer the New Forest.

G E Briscoe Eyre, in Evidence to 1875 Select Committee.

On entering the wood, the change of scene is startling and complete. The drooping boughs that veiled the entrance now conceal the approach, and a deep gloom succeeds to the open sunshine. A narrow band of light on either slope marks the limits of the grove; the dim space in front is broken only by the low, massive trunks and soaring limbs of great beech-trees, in every feature eloquent of antiquity. The expressive silence, the 'listening gloom,' and cloistral solitude, produce in the beholder a strange sense of mystery and awe.

G E Briscoe Eyre, 'The New Forest', A sketch from The Fortnightly Review, April 1st 1871.

When I want to feel at peace I walk only among the trees of the Forest, where the tracks of other feet are clearly defined and I know that I am in the world of human beings. In the heathlands, as I walk, the heather springs up again, resilient against the weight of a human body and I can become completely detached from other people. Here I can lose myself physically in a trackless waste and so find myself spiritually renewing an unknown source of strength within myself.

Sybis Leek, A Fool and a Tree, 1964.

Every time of year has its own especial beauty. Winter reveals lichens that grow like grey fur on bare branches, mosses that clothe boles and limbs with vivid green, buds that show subtle difference of colour such as can only be seen in a smokeless district, and moorlands clad in sober vesture of dun brown. In spring the tender green of young leaves contrasts with the ruddy buds of backward beeches, the golden furze-brakes with the silver bloom of thorns and crab-apples, the rust-coloured catkins of sweet-gale with the withered bog-sedge. In summer the old woods are in heavy foliage, the thickets are wreathed with honeysuckle and crowded with bracken and foxgloves breast-high; the heather is in bloom, and the bogs are starred with cotton-grass and gilded with asphodel.

Heywood Sumner, A Guide to the New Forest, 1925.

Against this colourful background the landscape is unique in Britain in being populated by large free ranging animals. The New Forest ponies, which may be the descendants of the original wild ponies of the area, are the most widespread. They add movement and interest to any scene, whether being 'drifted' across open heathland in galloping herds, gathered beneath the shade of giant trees in the shelter of the woodland, or drinking at the streams. Other animals may also be seen though they are not as abundant. Cattle freely graze some of the lawns and heaths. In the pannage season in the autumn, pigs are let loose to root for mast and acorns and one can sometimes see pink piglets scampering beneath the trees, bringing an unusual touch of humour to the scene. Deer are also present but less easy to see as they live quietly in the woods. For many people, a drive through the New Forest with the opportunity to enjoy these animals, is the nearest they will ever get to the experience of seeing wild free roaming game in an African reserve, outside the artificial confines of a safari park.

While these large grazing animals are the most easily seen, the whole Forest contains a wealth of plant and animal life which is itself an integral part of the landscape as well as being of great interest and value in its own right. The woods, heaths, bogs, wet tussocky grassland and lawns provide an unusually varied and extensive range of habitats which is of outstanding ecological importance. In the woods an important range of insects, lichens and birds can be found. The heaths and bogs support a great variety of plants, and birds such as Dartford warblers, nightjars and stonechats, while the tussocky grass and heathland provides a breeding ground for redshank and snipe, and for curlew, which are more often heard rather than seen. Birds of prey breed in the woods and hunt over the heaths.

Many of these aspects of the landscape would have been quite familiar to Gilpin two hundred years ago. He would, however, have been somewhat taken aback by others. What, for example, would he have made of the towering stacks of the Fawley power station looming above the forest fringes to the east? And what would he have said about the effects of modern recreation on his picturesque forest scenery? Today the New Forest caters for more than seven million visitors a year. However well designed or discreetly located they are, the associated trappings of cars and car parks, tents and toilets, people and picnic sites, are now an integral part of the landscape. Even without the influence of recreation the Forest today is a very different place from two hundred years ago. Roads and railways have had a substantial effect and the effects of traffic are felt throughout the Forest. The Forest is now an active living and working environment for many people.

This then is the essence of the New Forest today. It is a landscape of contrasts - between the old and the new, the open and the enclosed, the colourful and the sombre, the peaceful and the crowded. It retains much of the picturesque beauty which so enchanted Gilpin in his day, and has roots much further back in medieval England; yet it is also a landscape of the twentieth century which, by its very nature, might almost be said to have been designed to suit modern tastes in recreation, and which supports a working economy of commoning and forestry as well as a thriving population in its villages and towns. To understand the contrasts, complexities and contradictions which epitomise the New Forest landscape we must examine it in greater detail and look at the influences which have shaped it.

You will see fallow deer with their spreading antlers, the smaller reddish-brown roe, the little spotted sika and if you are lucky, a massive red deer stag guarding his harem of hinds with their floppy ears and large eloquent eyes. Kingfishers gleam over the Forest streams, herons stalk the marshes, the large green and red woodpeckers tap insistently for termites against dead stumps, their calls echoing like laughter round the woods.

Anne-Marie Edwards, *The Unknown Forest*, 1981.

In England the top forest for tourism is the New Forest – two-thirds of it unenclosed, and all of it a 'site of special scientific interest'. A survival of medieval England, with 80 miles of river and ancient woodlands, plus deer, ponies and commoners' cattle grazing at will, offers visitors a very special experience. Added attractions include a reptiliary, ten waymarked walks, ornamental drives, bookable barbecue sites, and special sites for rallies of campers and caravanners.

Tony Aldous, in *Tourism in Action* 1985.

3. Forces which have shaped the landscape

As with every landscape, the physical influences of geology, soils and the form of the ground have had the most profound influence in shaping the scenery of the New Forest. But of equal importance in this case are the historical influences of many centuries of common grazing and woodland management, and the more recent history of conservation and recreation.

Physical influences

Geologically the New Forest lies in a central position in a formation known as the Hampshire Basin. This is a down-fold in the underlying chalk strata which quite recently in geological time was filled by sedimentation from a succession of shallow seas, freshwater lakes and rivers. Each period of sedimentation left a different type of deposit, so forming a series of overlying layers of sands and clays. Subsequent folding and tilting caused the older deposits to be exposed in the northern parts of the basin while the younger ones are exposed in the south, and intermediary deposits are exposed in between. The sediments were later raised above sea level as a flat plateau and in a later period were covered by a capping of gravels. The geological deposits which underlie the New Forest are therefore soft sedimentary sand and clays overlain by gravel.

These sands and clays produce mainly poor acid soils, but the ones which are of marine origin tend to produce slightly better, less acid soils. As they are found mainly in the southern part of the Forest this means that, in general, the soils are poorer in the north and better in the south. Interaction with climate, with vegetation and with land use has resulted in a spectrum of soils which ranges from poor acid podzols, to better brown earths, to brown forest soils, to wet peat and river alluvium in the valley bottoms.

After these geological deposits were laid down, erosion acted to create the landforms which exist today. Changes in sea level, linked with formation of the gravel capping, produced a flight of huge terraces which are still visible today running from the high land in the north west down to the Solent shore. These terraces are an important feature in the landscape today.

The gravel strata protected the underlying layers from much of the eroding effect of water but once the gravel cap was broken the soft underlying deposits were easily eroded. In northern parts of the Forest the streams run westwards to the River Avon and, because of their relatively steep gradient, they have considerable power to wear away underlying rocks. This, coupled with the higher land in the north, means that quite steep sided 'U'-shaped valleys have been formed, separated by narrow flat topped plateaus. By contrast, in the central and southern parts of the Forest, the land is lower lying and the streams draining south to the Solent have a greater distance to travel and are less eroding. As a result the valleys are much broader and shallower and the landform consists primarily of flat plains.

None of these land forms are dramatic, for the New Forest is what has been called 'soft rock' country where the nature of the ground is much more subtle than in landscapes formed of hard rock. The overlaying of different strata had particular effects on water flow. Springs emerged between strata of different hardness and wore away the valley sides to form smaller side valleys. Seepage along these junctions also caused slumping into terraces or steps. Although the area was not covered by an ice cap in glacial times it was probably tundra, with the ground affected to some depth by permafrost. These 'peri-glacial' conditions caused many even more subtle changes in the land. There were contortions in the upper layers. The annual cycle of freeze and thaw, with resultant flooding, was very effective in eroding the valleys and formed characteristic features such as the 'dells' which were hollowed out of some of the steeper valley

None of the landforms are dramatic except for the 'U'-shaped valleys in the open heaths of the northern Forest.

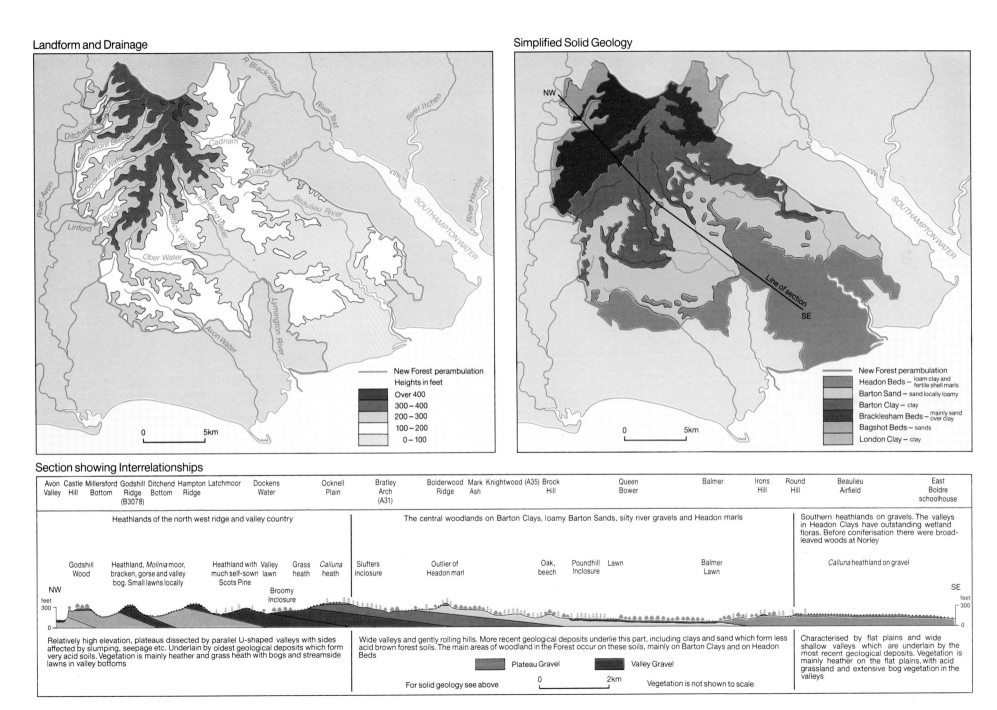

Figure 1. Geology, landform and vegetation

11

With its long and exceedingly well-documented history the Forest is unique in that the scene we see today contains so many visible clues and reminders of that history.

sides. All these features, of terraces, steps, side valleys, dells and springs, are all visible today along valley sides, especially in the north where the landscape is open rather than wooded. There is still much debate about the exact nature of the physical changes which have taken place over the centuries and the Forest is an important area for the study of these processes.

There are close relationships between topography, geology, soils and vegetation. One has only to look at the way in which the enclosed and settled lands are so closely linked with the distribution of better quality soils to begin to see this. The forest can be divided very broadly into three parts. The northern part is characterised by its relatively high elevation (including the highest point of Bramshaw Telegraph at 418 feet), and by the presence of five parallel 'U'-shaped valleys separated by fairly flat plateaus. The sides of these valleys show evidence of slumping, seepage and other similar effects. Underlying this area are the oldest geological deposits which have produced the most acid and impoverished soils. On the plateaus these support predominantly heathland vegetation but down the valley sides there is a mosaic of wet heath, acid grassland and some woodland.

In the central part the land is lower lying and the valleys are wider, less pronounced and separated by undulating plateaus. The geological deposits are more recent than in the north and include clays and sands which form the better quality brown forest soils. These soils are well suited to tree growth and for this reason much of the woodland, including both the Ancient and Ornamental Woodlands and the Timber Inclosures, occurs in this central part of the Forest.

In the southern part the land is very low lying, and streams have had little eroding effect, so that flat plains are the most characteristic feature. Here the most recent geological deposits occur, and large areas are also underlain by the superficial plateau gravels. The pattern of soils is complex with some better quality loams and clays supporting grassland, while the poorer sandy soils support heathland. The wide valleys contain accumulations of peat which support bog vegetation.

This is a very simplified picture of what are inevitably very complex relationships. The pattern is illustrated by the sketch maps and section in Figure 1. Other factors also have an important influence on the landscape. Peat is widespread throughout the Forest and where drainage is poor it leads to the formation of bogs in valleys and low lying depressions. The character of the peat varies according to the nature of the surrounding land and the minerals which are washed down from it. So, for example, the bogs in the north are more acidic than those in the central and southern areas. In some valleys relatively well drained alluvium, washed down by the streams takes the place of peat. It forms some of the best soils in the Forest and supports fertile streamside grass 'lawns'.

Historical influences

With its long and exceedingly well documented history, the New Forest is unique in that the scene we see today contains so many visible clues and reminders of that history. Put simply, the Forest is a surprisingly intact remnant of a medieval hunting forest. But there is much more to it than that. John Wise, writing in 1863 in his book, *The New Forest: Its History and Scenery*, puts the historical perspective most aptly when he says:

"The New Forest is, perhaps, as good an example as could be wished of what has been said of English scenery and its connection with our history. It remains, after some eight hundred years, still the New Forest. True its boundaries are smaller, but the main features are the same as on the day when first afforested by the Conqueror. The names of its woods and streams and plains are the same . . . the New Forest still stands full of old associations with, and memories of the past."

. . . this part of the Forest gives a curious impression of being at least as high as the thousand-foot Uplands of Dartmoor. Possibly the reason is partly the sudden rise of two hundred feet from the valley of the Avon, and partly the extent of the view. From Broomy walk the wide river valley seems far below and it is possible to look away for fifteen-miles north westwards to the rolling chalk hills of Wiltshire and Dorset.

Ralph Wightman, *The Wessex Heathland*, 1953.

. . . here we have long rolling hills, capped with plateau gravel and clothed with heather, fern, and furze, worn into five parallel ridges and furrows by streams that trickle in dry, and rush in wet weather, down gravelly courses to the broad valley of the Avon. Here and there the hills are covered with thickets of holly, thorn, yew, and crab-apple; with old woods of oak, beech, yew, holly, thorn, and whitebeam; and with enclosures of Scots pine, larch, oak, and sweet chestnut. But the main features of our side of the New Forest are heather uplands, winding moorland streams, and scattered woods.

Heywood Sumner, *The Book of Gorley*, 1910.

It is not to be forgotten that the soil of the New Forest is of a varied character; several different soils are found in close proximity; the trees adapt themselves to the soil that suits them, and this gives the beautiful varied character to the scenery which the Forest possesses.

Memorandum of a visit to certain old woods of the New Forest. Esdaile, Lovell and Montagu of Beaulieu, 1899.

I suppose this is what strikes most persons when they first come into the New Forest, – a sense that amidst all the change which is going forward, here is one place which is little altered. This is what gives it its greatest charm, – the beauty of wildness and desolateness, broken by glimpses of cultivated fields, and the smoke of unseen homesteads among the woods.

J R Wise, *The New Forest : Its History and Scenery*, First Edition, 1863.

The fact that such associations still have relevance for those who visit the Forest today is indicated by the emphasis placed on the historical aspects in popular literature such as the Ordnance Survey's 1983 *Leisure Guide* which suggests that:

> "the appeal of the New Forest must largely be based on its status as a surviving slice of medieval, if not merrie, England. Its place names — Ferny Knap, Dame's Slough, King's Garn Gutter Inclosure — awaken a buried sense of times gone by".

The earliest periods in the history of the landscape, before written records existed, are not clearly understood but it is believed that there is enormous potential in the Forest for the discovery of evidence about the pre-Norman period. At present, archaeological evidence and analysis of pollen in the soil suggest some form of Bronze Age occupation, with a large number of barrows and signs of shifting cultivation of nearby land. Early pollen records indicated that at one time the area was more extensively wooded, with a greater variety of trees present. It is thought that the extent of Bronze Age occupation, with its associated farming practices, eventually led to a degrading of the soils and the spread of heathland where formerly there had been woodland. A number of hillforts also suggest Iron Age occupation which, because of the soil degradation, was either peripheral to the Forest or confined to areas of better quality soil. There is also evidence of an extensive Romano-British pottery industry using the good local pottery clays.

But the real history of the Forest landscape begins after the Norman Conquest. At this time the landscape was a waste of heath and furze known as Ytene (meaning 'of the Jutes'). Evidence from other Juteish settlements suggests that there would at this time have been communal rights over the heaths and woodland allowing for the use of deer, timber, browse and other Forest produce. William the Conqueror then claimed the land from his nearby seat in Winchester, as a Royal Forest and hunting ground and changed its name to 'Nova Foresta', the New Forest. Over the next nine hundred years the contrast which we see today between the open and wooded parts of the landscape, is mirrored in the tensions between the two main and contrasting threads of historical land use, namely the grazing of deer and stock on the open forest and the management and enclosure of the woodlands for timber on a large scale since 1700. The rapid growth of recreation in the Forest since Victorian times is a third factor which has had a profound influence on the landscape in the latter part of the century.

After William had claimed the land, in a year generally thought to be 1079, a perambulation or boundary was eventually defined and within this area (which was more extensive than today's perambulation) Forest Law was applied. The purpose of Forest Law was, in effect, to manage the Forest in such a way as to carry the largest possible stock of deer whilst maintaining 'the comeliness and beauty of the Vert'. It might in many ways be regarded as an early form of management plan and had a profound effect on the Forest which is still apparent today. Before afforestation, animals could be freely grazed on the common wastes but Forest Law protected the wild animals, especially the deer, and brought the common grazing under control. Grazing animals had to be removed for more than six months of the year. Timber and undergrowth were protected as cover for deer and fencing was prohibited so that there would be no interference with their movement. Fruit or mast bearing trees were protected as 'silva fruticosa' (fruitful trees) and such trees, including oak, beech, holly, blackthorn, hawthorn, crab, rowan and whitebeam are abundant today while others not bearing fruit have declined. The administration of Forest Law brought with it the creation of special bodies and offices, notably the Courts of Swainmote and Attachment which were presided over by the Verderers to preserve the interests of the Crown.

The depasturing of commoner's animals continues today, although stocking levels have changed considerably. In the eighteenth century between 7,000 and 9,000 animals are estimated to have been turned out, with similar numbers of deer grazing and browsing in the forest. Numbers today are much reduced

Out on the heath too, there are sounds and scents to haunt your memory: larks soaring and singing even on grey days, heather and gorse smelling as rich as honey, the sharp tang of the gold-withey (or bog myrtle) as you brush past it by the streams. You will be rewarded by spreading views, west over the Avon valley to the Wiltshire Downs, south to the curving line of the Isle of Wight hills. And here you will feel close to the Forest's history as you pass tumuli or burial mounds raised by Britons a thousand years before the birth of Christ, and climb the embankments of Iron Age hill forts which dominated the hill tops when the Romans landed.

Anne-Marie Edwards, *The Unknown Forest*, 1981.

Queens Bower

Heywood Sumner etching from J R Wise, The New Forest, *1895 edition*

The Ancient and Ornamental Woods retain a sense of great beauty as well as embodying the history of Forest use and management.

Grazing animals contribute to the picturesque scenery of the Forest, both in their own right, and in the effect of their grazing in maintaining the open forest.

16

— 4,849 cattle and ponies were turned out on the Forest and the adjacent commons in 1984, and the deer population in recent years has been estimated to lie somewhere between 1,100 and 1,400. These grazing animals make an enormous contribution to the picturesque scenery of the Forest, both in their own right, and in the effect of their grazing in maintaining some form of balance between the open and wooded parts of the landscape. At the same time the traditional pastoral economy of commoning is a unique feature of the Forest and the Commoners have been a strong and cohesive social force in the Forest community with a character and history which is peculiarly their own. Continuation of the landscape in anything like its present form is dependent to a large degree upon the maintenance of a healthy commoning economy.

Forest Law was observed to varying degrees over the centuries, but gradually came to be much more concerned with the needs of the Commoners than with those of the Crown. It formally disappeared in 1971. The original Courts have been reorganised and the Verderer's Court now deals with many matters relating to the exercise of common rights in the Forest, including administration of their own bylaws, and generally with maintaining the traditional character of the Forest. Although functions have changed, much of the original medieval administration of the Forest remains, and is vital in maintaining the links between the New Forest today and the history and traditions which have formed it.

After the fifteenth century, and some four hundred years of Forest Law, the balance began to change from the conservation of deer to the production of timber from the Forest, mainly because of the needs of ship building. This meant that areas of the Forest must be enclosed against grazing and browsing by deer and commoner's animals. Acts of Parliament gradually increased the extent of permitted enclosure beginning with the 1851 New Forest Deer Removal Act. This ended the Crown's interest in deer conservation by requiring the removal of the animals, thereby increasing the availability of grazing for the Commoners' animals. It also allowed the Crown to enclose a further 10,000 acres for timber, on top of the 6,000 acres already enclosed. The Commissioners of Woods at the time chose to interpret this as a 'rolling power' of enclosure which, if exercised, could eventually have led to the planting of virtually the whole Forest.

Public outcry at the effects of this on the Commoner's rights and on the picturesque scenery of the Forest, which at the time was widely recognised and very highly valued, led to Select Committees of Inquiry of the House of Lords in 1868 and Commons in 1875. The resulting New Forest Act of 1877 limited the Crown's powers of enclosure to those areas which were, or had been, enclosed at the time the Act was passed, thereby effectively establishing some form of balance between the Commoners' needs for open forest grazing and the Crown's desire for timber. The balance between open land and enclosed woodland, which is such a vital part of the scenery, was ensured.

Although the extent of enclosure was fixed in the Act (and extended in a later (1949) Act) the tensions continued. The Commoners continued to be concerned by encroachments on, or lack of management of, common grazing land. The First World War brought heavy demands for timber at a time when improved access was seeing a growth in the popularity of the Forest and a wider appreciation of its beauty. Soon afterwards, in 1923, the Forestry Commission assumed responsibility for the Forest, on behalf of the Crown, and the debate switched to being concerned less with the area of enclosure than with the way in which the woodlands were managed and the types of trees planted. This was already a matter of disagreement in the nineteenth century, but it now became a major controversy which has continued to varying degrees over the years. New committees were established to look into this and other problems which faced the Forest, and new Acts were passed in 1949 and 1964 to help the New Forest to react to the changing demands of modern society.

Obviously the preservation of the picturesque scenery of the Forest is of paramount importance. But that is not all: the uniqueness of the Forest does not rest in its scenery alone. There are the ponies, for instance, and the Commoners' other animals which are not only picturesque in themselves but are, as will be shown later, amongst the actual architects of the characteristic scenery of the Forest.

Forestry Commission, *Protection of the New Forest : Report of the Committee of Planning Officers 1938-1939*, HMSO, 1939.

Instead of small woods picturesquely distributed over the whole forest, plantations measurable by the square mile, and closely adjacent to each other, occupy its most beautiful hollows. In such places the native woodland has been completely swept away, and the old ornamental woods have gone to drug the timber market. Many a grassy valley and cattle-studded lawn has disappeared for ever beneath a sombre sea of Scotch fir. The pastures thus planted are destroyed, the old winding ways are filled with trees and intersected by indelible trenches, the new rides are laid out on no intelligible principle of convenience or picturesqueness, so that the plantations, when again thrown open to the public and the commoners, will offer neither free-passage, pasturage, nor beauty.

G E Briscoe Eyre, 'The New Forest', A sketch from *The Fortnightly Review*, April 1st 1871.

Another milestone in the Forest's history was the Act's recognition of the amenity value of the area as a place of great beauty. This evolution of the official attitude to the Forest – from early game park to timber-producing woodland to a precious part of our national heritage – is interesting to trace, for it reflects the growth and increasing sophistication in our own society from medieval to modern times.

O S *New Forest Leisure Guide*, 1983.

. . . the great beauty of the forest is its distinctive character, that a great part of it has been, as far as I understand, planted naturally and not artifically. Such a natural forest always possesses a kind of beauty which a formed plantation does not. The beauty of the forest is the creation of generations.

Henry Fawcett, in Evidence to 1875 Select Committee.

In the meantime, the Second World War had also had a major impact on the landscape. Wartime airfields were located at Stoney Cross, Holmsley and Beaulieu Heath and, although now substantially reclaimed, some of the hard surfacing still remains as evidence of this activity. The needs of war also allowed the first deliberate attempt to improve the agricultural productivity of the Forest. The New Forest Pastoral Development Scheme began experimental creation of improved grazings in 1941. The programme continued between 1944 and 1952 and eventually 900 acres were reseeded in fifteen different places.

In 1971 the Forestry Commission was given a mandate by the Minister of Agriculture, Fisheries and Food, which firmly established that "the New Forest is to be regarded as a national heritage and priority given to the conservation of its traditional character". This led to the preparation of a management plan to cover the decade from 1972-81, in order to put the mandate into effect. A second plan, covering the period 1982-91, has now superseded this. In this latest plan the mandate has been translated into a general management objective for the whole Forest which aims "to maintain and safeguard the traditional character and statutory uses of the whole Forest, without conflict with its ecological stability and diversity".

This management objective gives further recognition to the outstanding ecological value of the whole complex of habitats in the New Forest. This importance had been increasingly recognised in the 1950s and 60s and there was much consultation with the Nature Conservancy at that time. This was formalised by signature of a Minute of Intent in 1969 which recognised the Forest as having status equivalent to a national nature reserve and required consultation between the Forestry Commission and the Nature Conservancy. Ecological factors were given added weight by the designation of the Forest as a site of special scientific interest (SSSI) in 1974, and by inclusion of its ancient woodlands, heathlands and bogs as outstanding representatives of their type in the comprehensive review of nature conservation sites carried out in Britain in the 1970s.

At the same time as the ecological value of the Forest was being recognised, its popularity as a place to visit for recreation was growing rapidly. The numbers of visitors and cars, and the freedom which existed at that time to drive off the roads in many parts of the open Forest, were beginning to cause unacceptable damage. In 1970, just prior to the introduction of the mandate, a report on the Conservation of the New Forest was prepared by a joint working party involving the Forestry Commission, Hampshire County Council, New Forest Rural District Council, Ringwood and Fordingbridge Rural District Councils, the Nature Conservancy and the Verderers. The proposals put forward were intended to protect the wildlife, landscape and historical value of the Forest from the growing pressures of day visitors. They have provided the framework for all the subsequent development of facilities for visitors.

Recreation has thus been a major factor in the recent history of the Forest and has rightly received considerable attention in efforts to find a balance between conservation and the needs of those who wish to enjoy the Forest. Today attention is increasingly turning to the future of commoning as an integral part of the Forest system. Changes in population, work patterns and land ownership may eventually lead to a decline in the practice of commoning with serious consequences for the landscape and for the traditions and culture of the Forest. The way in which such changes are met may well be the latest chapter in the evolution of the Forest landscape.

The phenomenon of recreation on a vast and previously undreamed-of scale has posed a major threat to the New Forest. And a phenomenon it is. In the summer of 1965, the New Forest received 85,000 campers. That figure has now risen to 800,000. The campers, of course, are merely in the vanguard of a much larger army of day visitors and holidaymakers, whose numbers total six-and-one-half to seven million per annum.

O S *New Forest Leisure Guide*, 1983.

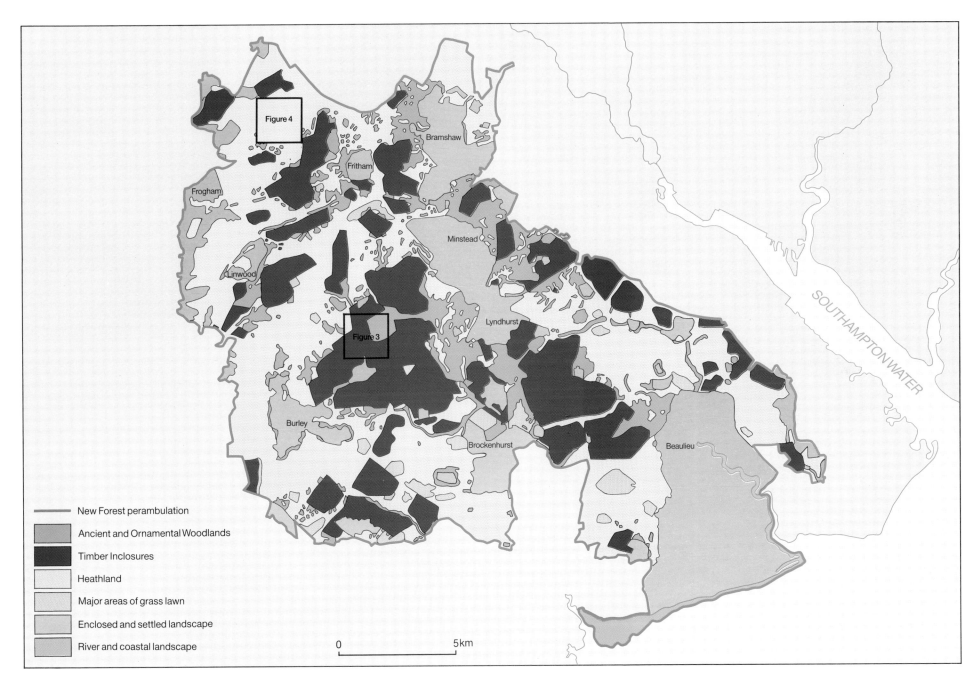

Figure 2. The mosaic of landscape elements.

Legend:
- New Forest perambulation
- Ancient and Ornamental Woodlands
- Timber Inclosures
- Heathland
- Major areas of grass lawn
- Enclosed and settled landscape
- River and coastal landscape

Map labels: Figure 4, Bramshaw, Fritham, Frogham, Minstead, Linwood, Lyndhurst, Burley, Figure 3, Brockenhurst, Beaulieu, SOUTHAMPTON WATER

0 5km

Figure 3 Woodland landscapes

Ancient and Ornamental Woodlands

Largest remaining area of primary woodland in lowland Britain. Have escaped serious modification over last 500 years. Mainly oak or beech or a mixture of the two, usually with an understorey of holly. Many old trees and dead timber. Also include mixed woods with ash, yew, birch as well as clumps of holly called "hats".

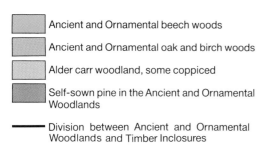

Ancient and Ornamental beech woods

Ancient and Ornamental oak and birch woods

Alder carr woodland, some coppiced

Self-sown pine in the Ancient and Ornamental Woodlands

Division between Ancient and Ornamental Woodlands and Timber Inclosures

Uncoloured areas are not part of the woodland landscapes

Timber Inclosures

The great majority of Inclosures have been formed since 1698 with the main period of planting between 1808 and 1870, and a further 2000 acres planted since the 1949 Act. The early Inclosures were of oak but extensive areas of conifers were planted after the 1851 Deer Removal Act. Most Inclosures now show diversity of species and age of trees. Clear felling of large areas is now avoided and natural regeneration used where possible.

Plantation oak or beech, dating from 1800 – 1850

Mixed oak or beech plantations dating from 1810 – 1830

Mixed plantations of conifers with oak and beech

Conifer plantations including Scots pine, Corsican pine, Douglas fir, Norway spruce, hybrid larch, western hemlock etc.

Forestry Commission compartment boundary

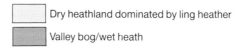
0   500m

Figure 4 Open landscapes

Grassland

Includes natural grass "lawns" (on rich alluvial soils alongside streams on valley floors, and in the woodland glades, on verges and village greens and around pools), re-seeded areas including reclaimed war-time airfields, and natural acid grassland with bristle bent and purple moor grass, often invaded by bracken and gorse.

Streamside grass lawns

Acidic grassland with purple moor grass, bracken and gorse

Scots pine has invaded both grassland and heathland areas and patches of seedlings, clumps of young trees or groves of mature trees are widespread in the open forest

Uncoloured areas are not part of the open landscapes

0   500m

Heathland and valley bogs

Dry heathland occurs on poor sandy soils and consists of ling heather, bell heather, cross-leaved heath, dwarf gorse and purple moor grass in various combinations, with gorse in disturbed areas. Valley bogs and wet heath occurs on accumulations of peat in valleys and low basins and often has alder carr or bog myrtle by the central stream with other bog vegetation beyond.

Dry heathland dominated by ling heather

Valley bog/wet heath

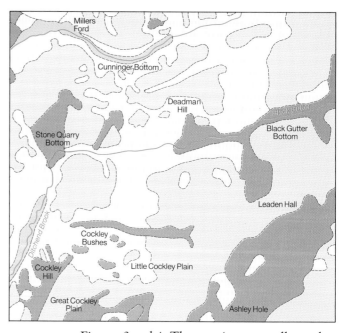

Figures 3 and 4. The mosaic on a smaller scale.

4. The character of the landscape

The New Forest landscape today is a most complex mosaic combining a number of different elements. This gives it its distinctive character. It can be viewed at two levels. At a general level it consists of open spaces, either of heathland or grass, set alongside the masses of woodland, both the irregular Ancient and Ornamental Woodlands and the more regular fenced outlines of the planted Timber Inclosures. The way that these elements are disposed in relation to each other and to the contrasting areas of enclosed land and settlements and the river and coastal areas, is illustrated in Figure 2.

Examined more closely, the landscape reveals an even more diverse and complex mosaic. The heathland areas include wet bogs, bracken, gorse and tracts of heather. The grassland may be naturally fertile streamside or woodland lawns, artificially re-seeded leys or reclaimed airfields or may be acid grassland occurring with heathland. The Timber Inclosures may include old deciduous woodlands similar to those which are unenclosed, mature deciduous plantations, younger deciduous plantations, coniferous plantations or mixtures of both deciduous and coniferous trees. The Ancient and Ornamental Woodlands may consist predominantly of oak, or beech, or a mixture of both, but in stream valleys they are mainly alder or willow and there is also a growing area of naturally seeded Scots pine woodland. The complexity of the mosaic at this more detailed level is illustrated by Figure 3 which shows a representative area of woodland and Figure 4 which shows an area of open land.

There are enormous variations in the character of the landscape, depending upon the exact combination and disposition of all these elements in any one place. Nevertheless it is possible to identify five basic types of landscape with a clearly discernible character. They are woodland landscapes, found within the Ancient and Ornamental Woodlands and Timber Inclosures; open landscapes, found in the large open areas of heathland or lawn where woodland edges are not prominent; edge landscapes where open land, both heaths and lawns, and woodlands combine to form a diverse and highly attractive scene; enclosed landscapes which consist mainly of enclosed and settled land; and river and coastal landscapes.

Woodland landscapes are what Gilpin meant when he referred to "forest scenery as a foreground", meaning "the appearance which its woods present when we approach their skirts or invade their recesses". This enclosed scenery is found within every wooded area of the forest, but because the woodlands are concentrated on the better soils, it is found particularly in the central mass of woodlands surrounding Lyndhurst and Brockenhurst. Such woodland scenery is in itself highly varied in character. The Ancient and Ornamental Woodlands of the open forest, together with the small remnants of the original ancient woodland which are now incorporated within the Timber Inclosures, undoubtedly provide some of the most attractive woodland scenery in the Forest, and lie at the heart of Gilpin's vision of picturesque sylvan scenery.

They consist mainly of oak woods or beech woods or a mixture of both. Their character comes firstly from the beauty of form of the many mature specimens of these trees which dominate the woodland canopy. Each has its own particular qualities. Many of the oaks have peen pollarded, by cutting the branches about six or ten feet above the ground when the trees are young, giving them strange, stunted and squat shapes. The beeches have also been pollarded in places, but more often they have grown naturally, producing tall graceful trees with smooth grey bark, long fine branches and delicate leaves. Many different age groups are present and the natural way in which trees of different ages are disposed together creates a scene of great interest. This is heightened by variations in the ground; by the small

No fence or boundary marks the transition from heath to forest. The river slips from the common between clumps of holly and single waving birches, winds down a glade and in a few yards is lost to sight among masses of oak, alder, ash and pines. Looking backwards towards the sunset along this borderland, the rugged outlines of the gorse and fir, and the broken and wind-swept hollies and thorns which fringe the full-fed forest, give to the scene an air of wildness and confusion in striking contrast to the serene tranquility which reigns within the solemn precincts of the wood. Ober Heath is an example of the forest moor enclosed by wooded hills.

C J Cornish, *The New Forest*, 1910

Much has been spoken and written on the beauty of the Forest in all its aspects. Except for a few necessary words we must confine our attention to certain dangers by which it is threatened. The woodlands are the main interest to most observers but there are times and seasons when the open heaths dominate the scene, for instance in the early summer when the bracken fronds are unfolding, in the late summer when the bell heather is followed by the ling, giving a colour to the heaths which is rare in the South of England, and in the autumn when the bracken changes colour in harmony with the changing colours of the woods.

Report of the New Forest Committee, 1947.

. . . as the grand simplicity of such scenery demands – the exquisite subtlety with which nature has blended method and caprice, order and disorder, tenderness and strength, and the exquisite proportion which nature has during the gliding centuries established between the open spaces – the heaths, lawns, greens, glades, and gladeways, – and the woods and shaggy woodland, a proportion which no art could reproduce, and invaluable in forming the taste of the observer.

New Forest Exhibition Catalogue, 1875.

The Forest, under the division of wood, pasturage and heath, presents itself to us as a picturesque in a double view – as the scenery of a fore-ground and as the scenery of a distance.

Rev W Gilpin, *Remarks on Forest Scenery*, 1791.

A pool of water too is a lucky incident. When it is shrouded with trees and reflects from its deep, black mirror the mossy branches of an oak, or other objects in its neighbourhood which have received a strong touch of sunshine, it never fails to please.

Rev W Gilpin, *Remarks on Forest Scenery*, 1791.

21

glades, lawns or areas of heathland within the woodland; by quiet meandering streams, with overhanging trees, sometimes emerging into grassy glades or forming still pools; by the dramatic forms of dead trees; and by the presence of grazing or browsing animals.

Changes in colour and in light, during the day and through the seasons, is an important factor in these woodland landscapes. The interplay of light on grey bark, on light green leaves, on dewy grass and on still water creates a constantly shifting scene. Sunrise and sunset can cast shades of golden light on the silvery grey trunks and branches of the beech trees, bringing a special air of mystery to the woods. There are striking contrasts in colour between the dark understorey of holly set against the grey trunks of beech or oak, and the dappling of fallen leaves on the green grass. Autumn brings the splendour of the turning leaves, while in winter the bare branches form an intricate lacework, silhouetted against the sky.

The Timber Inclosures, all of which are managed for the production of wood, vary widely in their character. Some involved the enclosure of deciduous woodland already in existence. Some of the earliest plantations of oak and beech, dating from the eighteenth century, resemble the Ancient and Ornamental Woodlands in character, to some extent. The next wave of enclosure and planting, in the early and mid-nineteenth century, consisted primarily of oak and has also produced some very varied and attractive woodland areas. A survey carried out in 1970 identified a considerable area of these mature hardwood Inclosures, as being of primary amenity value, equal to the Ancient and Ornamental Woodlands. They were described in the survey as follows:

"In contrast to the ancient and ornamental type of woodland, their beauty is formal; and where accompanied by undulating country intersected by streams or other natural features they form some of the finest and most characteristic woodland scenery of the Forest".

Elsewhere in the Timber Inclosures the woodland landscape is less striking. The younger deciduous woods still provide an appealing and varied scene, although the trees lack the grand form of the older Inclosures. The mixed Inclosures, combining oak or beech with conifers, can also form quite attractive landscapes. Conifer plantations first played a significant role in the Forest after the Deer Removal Act of 1851, when Scots pine was planted on a large scale. Today they occupy just over half of the total area of the Inclosures. The more sombre tones and regular forms of the trees provide quite a different scene compared with the deciduous, or even the mixed plantations. While they have their own character, these conifer plantations lack the picturesque qualities of colour, changing light, and variety of tree forms which are characteristic of the older deciduous woodlands. They cannot be said to epitomise the New Forest landscape, even though certain coniferous areas do have their own special value, notably the specimen trees which form the ornamental drive, and the wonderful stand of Douglas fir, now 120 years old, at Boldrewood.

Inevitably, because the Inclosures are managed for timber production, they show more signs of human intervention than the natural communities of the Ancient and Ornamental Woodlands, which, by comparison, grow in a more random and disorderly manner. The large scale and regular fenced outlines of the Inclosures are also very different from the irregular and broken shapes of the unmanaged woods, as will be apparent from examination of Figure 2. Nevertheless, many of the deciduous plantations provide attractive landscapes, and the general system of forestry management, using relatively small scale felling, with natural regeneration contributing to replenishment as well as planting, is creating a diverse and interesting environment.

Then, too, there is that perpetual change which is ever going on, every shower and gleam of sunshine tinting the trees with colour from the tender tones of April and May, through the deep green of June, to the russet-red of autumn. Each season ever joins in this sweet conspiracy to oppress the woods with loveliness.

J R Wise, *The New Forest : Its History and Scenery*, First Edition, 1863.

Now we simply enjoy their natural beauty: the intricate patterns of their branches black against the winter sky, the subtle shading of green revealed in Spring sunlight, the deep russet red of last year's leaves beneath the beeches. These woods, particularly where oaks predominate, are loved by all wild creatures.

Anne-Marie Edwards, *The Unknown Forest*, A walkers guide, 1981.

Protection by bank, ditch and "hedge", (fence); varied tree-planting; natural re-generation by the up-growth of self-sown seedling trees; and the chances of Time; have all helped to produce the old woods that we now seek and admire – but we cannot look forward to such ultimate beauty arising from Inclosures that protect pure woods of Scots pine.

Heywood Sumner, *A Guide to the New Forest*, 1925.

Aesthetic objections are often raised against alien conifers. Certainly the serried ranks of any species grown under the monocultural, even-aged method can be far from attractive in their early stages but there are plenty of places where, except to a purist, mature conifers are aesthetically satisfying. Various cameos flit across the memory - the splendid conifers flanking the Ornamental Drive; a clump of pines on the skyline; a group of larches whose vivid green needles lighten the sombreness of nearby oaks; a V-shaped phalanx of spruce under snow creating a fairyland of delight.

O S *New Forest Leisure Guide*, 1983.

The woodland landscapes vary greatly in character from the historic Ancient and Ornamentals to the commercially managed Inclosures.

The open landscapes — the heathland and lawns — give a sense of freedom and openness quite different from the enclosure and shade of the woodlands. Their extent is unique in lowland Britain.

Open landscapes are the opposite, contrasting face of the New Forest. They give a sense of freedom and openness quite different from the enclosure and shade of the woodlands. A true feeling of open heathland landscape is only gained where there are uninterrupted tracts of heather, bog or other rough vegetation, which are not interrupted or bounded by woodland. This is surprisingly rare since the widespread distribution of the woodlands, and the extensive invasion by self sown Scots pines leaves relatively little heathland which is truly open. But such areas can be found, primarily in the northern part of the Forest, in the south west and in the south east. Each area has a different character resulting from the lie of the land, and the particular pattern of vegetation. Long views play an important part in these landscapes, whether they are over the Forest or the surrounding countryside.

In the north the 'upland' ridges and plateaus such as Deadman Hill and Hampton Ridge, offer many extensive views over open heathland; out from the Forest to the cultivated land of the surrounding chalk country; and south over endless receding skylines of woodland, towards the hills of the Isle of Wight beyond. The ridges and valleys offer a rolling prospect of bracken and heather, contrasting with the dark foliage and yellow flowers of gorse and brighter tones of the grass lawns in the valley bottoms.

In the south west, from Castle Hill on the western fringe of Burley, the land falls sharply away towards the River Avon in the west, in a continuous vista of the heathland and valley bog of Cranes Moor and Vales Moor. A dark cloak of heather covers most of the ground, with gorse in parts, but in the middle distance, swathes of purple moor grass provide a clear contrast, especially in the winter. Scots pines, growing singly and in clumps, punctuate the scene and form partial skylines in the distance. White flashes of bare and eroded ground create eye-catching incidents in the heather.

The plain of Beaulieu Heath in the south is different again. Here the ground is flat and gives no great sense of elevation. But the area is large and the continuous tracts of heather and gorse which cover most of it give a feeling of extent and provide a marked visual contrast to the areas of short green grass which exist on the site of the former airfield at the centre of the heath. There is extensive invasion by self-sown Scots pines in parts of this area. The trees are now growing, singly, in clumps, and in small woods, all of varying ages, and in some areas they are obscuring views over the open heath. Despite this, the heath can still, on occasions, provide long views to the Isle of Wight. The sunrises and sunsets are especially striking from this part of the Forest.

Each heathland scene has its own special qualities but they share certain characteristics. The valley bogs are a feature of all these areas, but are most extensive in the southern part. They have a distinctive vegetation, with purple moor grass, sedge and sphagnum moss dominating, depending upon the drainage conditions, and often with a central area, near the stream, with species such as bog myrtle, reed and other marsh species. Alder or willow trees usually mark the line of the water course. This characteristic vegetation is easily distinguished from the surrounding heathland and gives warning of the wet conditions underfoot.

It is the heathland parts of the Forest which demonstrate most clearly the importance of changing colour in the landscape. All the main types of vegetation show marked seasonal colour changes. From the summer green and the winter russet of the bracken, to the yellow flowering of the gorse in summer, to the purple flowering of heather in late summer and autumn — the range and combination of colour is endlessly varied. Because there is no woodland cover, the underlying features of the land are also more clearly exposed, whether they be the subtle features of land-form or the archaeological remains of former cultures. Above all, these landscapes share a sense of space, freedom of access and relative lack of human influence which is very rare in the south of England today.

This "wild and heathy scene" is neither lonesome nor dreary; its commanding height secures for it every charm that distant prospects, exhilarating air, and a sense of unlimited freedom can give.

G E Briscoe Eyre, 'The New Forest' A sketch from *The Fortnightly Review*, April 1st 1871.

If any one wishes to know the beauty of the Forest in autumn, let him see the view from the high ridge at Stoney-Cross. Here the air blows off the Wiltshire Downs finer and keener than anywhere else. Here, on all sides, stretch woods and moors. Here, in the latter end of August, the three heathers, one after another, cover every plain and holt with their crimson glory, mixed with the flashes of the dwarf furze.

J R Wise, *The New Forest : Its History and Scenery*, First Edition, 1863.

The whole area of Cranes Moor, Vales Moor and all the way up Verely Hill to Picket Post carries a network of paths . . . and a name: Smugglers Road. The sky was going from orange to red, the moorland from green to a powdery blue as it rolled away to the horizon. On the paths, figures moved, made vague and silhouettish, fuzzed at the edges by the sharpening light.

Peter Tate, *The New Forest Nine Hundred Years After*, 1979.

On Beaulieu Heath, there is a not a single tree, nothing but one vast stretch of heather, which late in the summer covers the ground with its crimson and amethyst. There is only one fault to be found with it, that when its glory is past it leaves so great a blank behind: its grey withered flowers and its grey scanty foliage forming such a contrast with its previous brightness and cheerfulness.

J R Wise, *The New Forest : Its History and Scenery*, First Edition, 1863.

It is often said that the best time to visit the forest is in the autumn, and if colour is a measure of beauty, then autumn it is. In the woods the deciduous trees add brightness to the sombre greens of the conifers, but for my choice it is the high plains, from almost all points still in view of the colourful woods, which are the grandest. Smooth sweeps of pink and purple heaths are the heralds of autumn, and in some years the colour hangs on until the swaying bracken turns brown and yellow, forming a brilliant foreground to the changing trees beyond.

W R Myers, in *The New Forest*, 1966.

The New Forest lawns are one of the most distinctive features of the landscape. They are open areas of short grazed grassland which are distinguished from the surrounding areas of heathland, bog and acid grassland by their relatively smooth uniform texture and their bright green colour. They generally occur on the richer soils and support a particular range of grass species often more commonly associated with cultivated grassland — hence their colour and the name 'lawns'. The quality of the grazing means that they often attract large numbers of ponies and views over lawns are frequently studded with grazing groups of animals.

Some lawns occur within the woodlands and along woodland streams, but many form part of the open landscapes. Naturally fertile lawns occur in the valley bottoms where there is richer alluvial soil. Here the bright green of the characteristically short cropped bent/fescue grassland provides a sharp contrast with the more muted, sombre tones of the surrounding heathland. Lawns in areas other than the valley bottoms have generally resulted from experimental cropping and re-seeding schemes which took place during and after the Second World War, and include the re-seeded wartime airfields at Stoney Cross, Holmsley and Beaulieu Heath. These areas are generally of a much larger and less intimate scale than the natural lawns. They lack the variation in texture and colour of the heathlands and the intimacy of the streamside lawns but they have their own characteristics, particularly their extent and uniformity and the number of animals attracted by the better quality grazing. But the lawns are still, as Gilpin observed, at their most attractive when they have an enclosing edge of woodland, scrub or gorse or lie in an intimate enclosed valley bottom.

Edge landscapes, where open landscapes and woodland landscapes occur together, are a particularly important feature of the New Forest. Such edges occur widely throughout the Forest, thereby contributing significantly to the scenery. But perhaps more importantly they often create a scene which many find particularly attractive for, although we may not be aware of it, edges have great significance in our perception of our surroundings.

The majority of edge landscapes in the Forest are formed by the juxtaposition of woodland and open land, whether it be grass lawn or heathland. The exact nature and character of the edge depends on where we are when we see it and on the nature of the elements forming the edge. From the middle of a heath, the edge may take the form of a quite distant wooded horizon, while from a small streamside lawn it may be the enclosing woodlands immediately around. The edge may be between a coniferous woodland and a heath, a deciduous woodland and a grass lawn, or one of a variety of other combinations. There may be an abrupt change from one to the other, or a gradual transition. The edge may be straight and regular or curved and irregular.

Where woodland forms distant horizons, the exact nature of the edge is not especially important. The types of trees present are not usually discernible and it is simply the presence of a distant skyline which is striking. But when the edge is nearby, its nature is very important to the way in which it is perceived and enjoyed. Certain types of edge form especially attractive landscapes. They owe their attractiveness to a number of factors, but most importantly to the scale of the space enclosed by the edge and the nature of the junction. They generally occur where there is a gradual transition from woodland to open land, with small trees such as birch and lower shrubs, combining to gradually merge the woodland with the lawn or heath. Such a gentle transition is usually combined with a deciduous edge which is naturally undulating rather than straight.

When both these features occur around an open area of heath, or more particularly lawn, which is of an intimate scale, then some of the most pleasing and attractive scenes in the Forest can be found. Examples can be seen at the fringes of Balmer Lawn, and Ober Heath, at White Moor, at Dogwood and

The forest-lawn in itself is a mere field. It is only when adorned with the furniture of surrounding woods, that it produces its effect.

Rev W Gilpin, *Remarks on Forest Scenery*, 1791.

The slopes that connect the moorland with the timbered lowland partake of the vegetation of both, and form a debatable land between them, where descending tongues of heath interpenetrate the advancing wedges of rough woodland. The exquisite interchange of hill and dale, and the random wild-wood characteristic of this intermediate region, give to New Forest scenery its peculiar beauty.

G E Briscoe Eyre, 'The New Forest' A sketch from *The Fortnightly Review*, April 1st 1871.

We skirt and penetrate the recesses of the woods for the closer view, but we frequent the forest lawn and heath for the distant one. The beauty of those scenes depends, it is true, in a great degree, on the play, and irregularities of the ground; but chiefly it depends on the surrounding woods.

Rev W Gilpin, *Remarks on Forest Scenery*, 1791.

The edge landscapes — the meeting place between the open and enclosed landscapes — form some of the most attractive Forest scenes and are very popular with visitors.

*The enclosed landscapes are those which have been farmed and occupied for
centuries — pockets of cultivation and settlement, within the more natural
landscapes of the surrounding Forest.*

Harvest Slade Bottom, at Longslade Bottom and at Ragged Boys Hill. These areas, and many others, have a strikingly intimate scale and sense of enclosure. Where they are easily accessible, and especially where there is also a stream, they often attract large numbers of people. This type of edge would have been much more common in the forest in the eighteenth and nineteenth centuries before the major period of enclosure of woodlands. Then there was an even more complex mosaic of many small areas of old woodland interspersed with fragments of heath and grassland, creating a considerable extent of highly varied edge and intimate spaces. Enclosure obscured much of this pattern.

The enclosed landscapes of the Forest, which include the cultivated farmland and settlements, are quite different in character from the woodland and open landscapes. These are the areas which have been enclosed and settled over the centuries, either by encroachment on Crown land, by special grants from the Crown, or by enclosure under licence. Today they form pockets of cultivation and settlement within the more natural landscapes of the surrounding forest. They include individual large properties such as Rhinefield House, smaller forest villages like Burley, Bramshaw, Minstead, Fritham and East Boldre, and the larger settlements of Brockenhurst and Lyndhurst, as well as enclosed areas of farmland.

Many of the settlements retain a distinctive Forest character and are never far from the enclosing woodlands and the open heaths and lawns. Some of them are early settlements which pre-date the establishment of the Royal Forest, while others have been formed within it . The elements of the surrounding Forest landscape are echoed in the villages, with their wide grazed grass verges, holly scrub, and mature trees: the farmland often appears to have been literally carved out of the surrounding Forest. Many of the houses are of traditional style and construction — some in brick and tile, others in thatch and wash. Together with the open grass areas and surrounding woodland, they often form very attractive village scenes. This is not to say that the Forest settlements have been untouched by recent development. There has been a significant growth of new housing in the last decade, especially in the larger settlements of Brockenhurst and Lyndhurst, which has sometimes led to a breakdown of the normally close physical relationship between the villages and the surrounding Forest.

While much of the enclosed farmland has the slightly unkempt appearance often associated with small holdings, the farmland which occupies the southern area of the Forest is of a quite different character. This is a well maintained, traditional landscape, much of it belonging to the Beaulieu estate. There are large fields ploughed for crops, or under temporary pasture, woodland copses of oak, trimmed roadside and field hedges with hedgerow trees, brick and tile farmsteads and estate cottages and newly planted pine plantations and poplar groves. The atmosphere is one of order and careful management. Proximity to the sea brings its own influences and many of the trees have an asymmetrical, wind-swept look resulting from constant exposure to sea winds.

Water plays an important part in the landscape throughout the Forest. The streams, called 'gutters' in the north and 'waters' in the south, flow almost invisibly through the open heaths and bogs, meander through the lawns, and creep quietly through the woods, occasionally forming pebbly pools and beaches which delight the visitors. The occasional ponds, probably of man-made origin, also act as a magnet to visitors. But the New Forest's main river and coastal landscapes are found where the Beaulieu River runs south to the Solent, providing waterside scenes on a larger scale. The perambulation here includes the middle reaches of the river and the west bank of its lower reaches, together with the Solent foreshore west nearly to Lymington. The Beaulieu River, with its associated villages of Beaulieu and Buckler's Hard lies outside the main areas of Forest landscape, within the cultivated land of the Beaulieu Estate. Beaulieu itself is a major attraction for tourists because of the National Motor Museum, Lord Montagu's Palace

. . . Another forest-lawn, of much larger dimensions, presents itself. This is very spacious, well hung with wood and (what in all these scenes adds greatly to their beauty) adorned in various parts with woody promontories shooting into it, and clumps.

Rev W Gilpin, *Remarks on Forest Scenery*, 1791.

Nor must man and his works be overlooked in the typical forest scene. Men are needed in the maintenance of the Forest and their work is picturesque. The little hamlets where they live will lose their character if they become the week-end resorts of townsmen. Villages like Lyndhurst, Burley, Bank, Emery Down, Minstead and Bramshaw are definitely to be counted amongst the forest amenities which ought to be preserved.

Forestry Commission, *Protection of the New Forest : Report of the Committee of Planning Officers 1938-1939*, HMSO, 1939.

If the whole of the Forest was changed and Bramshaw remained unaltered it would be possible, mentally, to reconstruct the rest. There are the great oaks of Bramshaw Wood, the lawns opposite the Bell Inn, the tiny farms, the hidden brook in the trees at Bramble Hill, the roadside ponds where great sows wallow in the mud, the open heather of Furzley Common with its solitary tumulus called Stagbury Hill, and that smell of heathland which would tell a blind Forester when he had reached home.

Ralph Wightman, *The Wessex Heathland*, 1953.

The woods which run for miles along the river banks are perhaps equally ancient with the oldest in the forest – ancient, that is, as having always been wooded ground. But their character is wholly different. They are the woods of a manor, grown for profit, carefully tended, and full of the close and beautiful sous bois, or underwood, which in the forest has disappeared and left only the haut bois, or timber trees. The woods on the opposite bank have that "carded" look, like curly hair combed, which sea-breezes give to trees . . .

C J Cornish, *The New Forest*, 1910.

The Forest streams, too, still flow on the same, losing themselves in the woods, eddying round and round in the deep, dark, prison-pools of their own making, and then escaping over shallows and ledges of rolled pebbles, left dry in the summer, and on which the sunlight rests, and the shadows of the beeches play, but in the winter chafed by the torrent.

J R Wise, *The New Forest : Its History and Scenery*, First Edition, 1863.

Unlike so many of our rivers, the Beaulieu river with its wooded banks and reed-fringed saltings hasn't changed much with the centuries. It has seen quite a variety of boats of course — trading vessels in medieval times, warships in the eighteenth century, and now a multitude of yachts and dinghies — but it's still a beautiful river and very rich in wildlife.

Anne-Marie Edwards, *New Forest Walks*, 1982.

House and the associated attractions. The setting of the village on the banks of the broad impounded freshwater part of the river, the presence of the enclosing riverside woodlands, the tranquil waters of the river itself, the many boats moored upon it, and the most attractive groupings of buildings in stone, brick, tile and timber, all combine to create a scene which is much enjoyed by visitors.

Buckler's Hard too is a popular port of call, with its maritime museum, boating activity on the river and its wide traffic-free main street flanked by lines of brick and tile cottages. Between the two villages the banks are cloaked in overhanging woodlands of oak, broken occasionally by meadows spreading down to the edge of the bank. There are fringes of saltmarsh in the southern stretches of the river and reed beds and alder carr further north. These combine with the mudflats and the meandering river to create a river landscape of great interest and beauty, albeit of quite different character from the rest of the Forest.

The coastal area included within the perambulation provides an ever greater contrast. This is an open, flat landscape, exposed to the full force of winds off the sea, and giving views across the Solent to the Isle of Wight. Between Lymington and Gull Island there are areas of saltmarsh and reed beds, shingle beaches, creeks, grazing marshes and coastal woodlands all rich in coastal flora and supporting large numbers of waders, wildfowl, gulls and other birds. Wooded skylines inland from the coast provide a reminder of the quite different Forest scenery which lies near at hand. Much of this sea shore area has limited access and is quiet and secluded, though also bleak and exposed.

Just a single street, bordered by lawns cropped short by Forest ponies, sloping down to the river between two rows of cottages built of rich red bricks. It is a pleasant homely village full of that unassuming charm so typical of the New Forest. There is nothing out of place here. The bricks and roof tiles made in the local brickworks a little upstream from Buckler's Hard blend harmoniously with the surrounding woodlands.

Anne-Marie Edwards, *New Forest Walks*, 1982.

Thus we finished our voyage up the River of Beaulieu which in a course of near three leagues from the sea, forms about five or six grand sweeps. The simple idea it presents throughout is that of a winding tide river flowing up a woody uninhabited country.

Rev W Gilpin, *Remarks on Forest Scenery*, 1791.

The landward slant of "bustle-headed" trees tells of prevailing sea winds, the stream estuaries tell of neighbouring tides, and the disused salterns in marshy flats, of a sea-water industry. Here the wayfarer arrives at a natural boundary of the Forest – the Solent.

Heywood Sumner, *A Guide to the New Forest*, 1925.

5. Change in the New Forest landscape

The landscape of the New Forest as we see it today is the product of interactions between natural and human influences over many centuries. It is what historians might call a 'palimpsest'or an overlaying of evidence from many different ages. For this reason it provides an admirable demonstration of the many complex interactions which shape a landscape. But such change is not purely a matter of history because the New Forest continues to be a dynamic landscape, evolving under the influence of contemporary land use and management. The changes affecting the Forest landscape today vary from the subtle and imperceptible, to the small scale and incremental, to the sudden and dramatic.

The most subtle and imperceptible changes arise from the natural dynamics of the vegetation. Forest grazing by Commoner's animals and by deer prevents the normal succession from open grass or heathland

In times of prosperous agriculture or heavy stocking with deer, the establishment of young trees was suppressed, until the number of browsing animals again fell. Certainly from the scenic point of view, this ebb and flow of regeneration produced many of the characteristic beauties of the Forest's woods, and was in no way detrimental. On a more limited scale, the competition between individual trees, twisting and distorting each other's forms in the perpetual struggle for light and space, created the very essence of the woodland scene.

A Pasmore, *Verderers of the New Forest*, c.1977.

Water plays an important part in the landscape whether in the form of 'gutters' or 'waters' flowing through the woods or open Forest, or the larger scale scenes along the Beaulieu River or the salt marshes of the Solent shore.

Change in the landscape can be of a subtle and incremental kind arising from the natural dynamics of the vegetation — pine, birch and scrub invasion — or more dramatic where lawns are improved or conifer plantations established.

to scrub and woodland, and so preserves the balance between the open landscape and the woodlands and maintains the all-important 'edge' landscapes. But the balance is a fine one and easily disturbed. If the number of grazing animals declines, scrub and woodland will spread, at the expense of open lawns and heathland. If stock numbers increase and grazing pressure is too high, some species of flora and fauna may not survive.

In addition to the level and distribution of grazing, the nature of the open forest landscape is also affected by planned intervention. The balance between natural and artificially re-seeded lawns, bog vegetation, heather, bracken, gorse and other scrub is influenced by decisions on the extent of cutting and burning of heathland, the removal of bracken, drainage of wet areas, and re-seeding and improvement of lawns and other grassland. Such decisions are finely balanced since they must respect the interests of the Commoners, of those concerned for the conservation of the New Forest, and of those who visit the Forest for recreation. Since the War there has been some increase in grassland resulting from the restoration of wartime encroachments, from improvements and from grazing strips around the post-war Inclosures, but there have also been losses to recreation and to the spread of scrub and bog. The management plan drawn up by the Forestry Commission for the period from 1982 to 1991 suggests that existing lawns may be improved and drainage restored, that some areas of bracken and rough grassland may be improved and that cutting and burning of the open forest will continue to an agreed programme.

Undoubtedly there will continue to be debate about the extent of such intervention and about where and how it should be carried out. It is however quite clear that such management decisions will become increasingly important. There is no doubt that the future of the New Forest landscape is inextricably bound up with the future of the Commoners and their grazing animals. Social and economic pressures may well lead, over the years, to a decline in commoning and to further encroachment of coarse herbage, scrub and woodland, so changing, perhaps irreversibly, the balance of open and enclosed landscapes which is such a feature of the New Forest.

Such a decline would certainly create an even greater need for intervention management to maintain the landscape, requiring a considerable increase in manpower and costs. However, it is the very diversity and complexity of the Forest landscape which makes land use plans not only very difficult to prepare but also of limited practical value. The balance of interests may be best served by clear objectives and an overall strategy, within which individual management decisions can be taken.

Such subtle changes in the vegetation of the open forest are perhaps best demonstrated by the invasion of open land by self-sown seedlings of Scots pine. It demonstrates clearly the nature of such change and the difficulty of striking an acceptable balance in deciding how much intervention there should be in such processes. Scots pine is first believed to have been planted in the New Forest in about 1820 but the problem of its invasion of the open forest became significant for the first time in the late nineteenth century. The pines planted in the Forest provided a source of seeds, and young trees sprang up around their fringes and in open areas of lawn and heathland. As soon as these changes became apparent there was a reaction against them, although those concerned with silviculture appear to have thought them desirable. By 1937 considerable areas of the Forest were reported to be infested and eventually a programme of clearance was begun.

But the invasion has continued and many areas of Scots pine have in themselves become important features of the landscape either as individual trees, attractive clumps in prominent positions, or as fringes to the Inclosures. A number are used as sites for car parks and picnic areas. Elsewhere though they are much less desirable. Their growth has reduced the grazing for stock, since ponies appear not to graze in

The great open heaths of the high grounds are a feature in themselves; they act, as it were, as a frame to the wooded portions, and were these to become covered with the self sown fir, of which there is serious danger, one of the most beautiful features of the forest would be destroyed, and all vistas of the woodland scenery and distant views would be obliterated. These seeding firs are also increasing greatly on the lower grounds, on the edges of lawns, and the courses of the streams, and eventually will block the views of the Woods, and thus destroying their effect.

Memorandum of a visit to certain old woods of the New Forest. Esdale, Lovell and Montagu of Beaulieu, 1899.

scrub pine areas. Lawns and heaths have been invaded, often obscuring the open character of the landscape, and many attractive open woodland glades have been filled in. In some cases the degree of penetration is so great as to cast doubt upon its future regeneration and status as broadleaved woodland. In recent years a broad consensus has been reached concerning the eradication of pine over large areas and their retention over a very limited area. An annual clearance programme now aims to make some inroads into the areas recommended for removal.

It is not only the open areas of the Forest which are subject to subtle changes of this sort. There has, for example, also been considerable debate about the extent to which the unenclosed Ancient and Ornamental Woodlands are naturally regenerating in the face of pressure of grazing by deer and commoners' animals. On one hand it has been suggested that grazing pressure has sometimes prevented regeneration of the woodlands leading to 'gaps' in the generation of trees present. On the other, survey has suggested that far from degenerating, the woodlands are regenerating vigorously and indeed have spread substantially in the last one hundred years, by invasion of areas which were formerly open heath or parkland. At present a policy of non-intervention is being pursued by the Forestry Commission so that over-mature and dead timber is not removed, and there is a reliance on natural regeneration to perpetuate the woodlands.

In the Timber Inclosures, change in the landscape is mainly dependent upon the silvicultural methods which are used. Over the last sixty years, the major change has been the conversion of many broadleaved Inclosures to coniferous plantations, so that today just over half of the statutory Inclosures are in fact coniferous. This represents a reduction in the coniferous proportion over the last ten years since the Minister's mandate was introduced in 1971. The new management plan, based on a 1982 mandate, proposes that the current overall balance between broadleaves and conifers will be maintained. This is likely to be the position for the immediately forseeable future although undoubtedly many will continue to argue that the eventual aim should be to return the Forest to a landscape primarily of broadleaved woodland, as it was in Gilpin's day.

Many of the more recent changes in the landscape have resulted from other pressures which are not directly related to the traditional uses and management of the Forest. These are the changes which result from development pressures of one form or another. Some have been sudden and dramatic — for example construction of the Esso oil refinery and the Fawley power stations has had a major visual impact on the eastern fringes of the New Forest landscape while the widening and fencing of the main A31 trunk road has effectively divided the northern part of the Forest from the southern part.

Others are on a smaller scale but are incremental in effect so that over the years they have combined together to bring about significant change. The growth in population in the surrounding areas and the increasing popularity of the Forest settlements as commuter bases has brought pressure for new housing. This has often served to consolidate the traditionally dispersed character of many Forest villages and changed the relationship between some settlements and the surrounding landscape, particularly at the edges of the Forest. Changing ownership of land and property has also brought changes, for example, the increase in the number of stable blocks as smallholdings are subdivided. These factors have caused a significant change to the climate within which commoning takes place, with less back up land for grazing off the Forest and a change in the character and aims of commoning. In addition to new building, the increasing population both inside and outside the Forest has generated more traffic, more noise and more demand for services and utilities whose provision can, in itself, bring yet more change to the landscape.

There are likely to be further pressures for development in the future. The interest of the oil industry in the New Forest led to a public inquiry into the sinking of a trial borehole and there are fears that there

Many recent changes in the landscape have been sudden, dramatic and urban in character — improved roads, powerlines and the provision of recreation facilities.

may be growing pressure to investigate and perhaps eventually to exploit on-shore oil resources lying beneath the Forest. Proposals to route a bypass around Lyndhurst are still under review and could have a major effect on an undisturbed area of the Forest. The planning authorities have done much to control the spread of new housing development but the pressures are still great, especially along the eastern fringes, and the social changes which fuel this pressure seem likely to continue.

Further changes have resulted from the rapid growth in the popularity of the New Forest for recreation since the War. The way that this pressure has been met and the changes which it has brought represent an important chapter in the recent history of the Forest. They are examined in more detail in the next section.

6. Recreation in the landscape

The enormous growth in the popularity of the New Forest as a place to visit for recreation has had a great effect in the period since the War. It deserves more detailed consideration for two reasons. Firstly, the sheer volume of people coming means that recreation, and the physical provision for it, has itself come to be an important feature of the landscape. Secondly, the way that people use and enjoy the Forest may give some clues as to what it is that they particularly like about it and help us to understand the importance of the landscape.

The New Forest has been recognised as an attractive place to visit since the mid-nineteenth century when the coming of the railway made it accessible to visitors from as far afield as London. But numbers of visitors then were relatively small and the Forest still belonged primarily to those who lived there — the Commoners, their animals and the Foresters. The growth of car ownership changed all this and by the late 1960s so many people were coming to the Forest that conflicts were arising and damage was being caused. In 1969, 3.5 million visits were estimated to have been made to the Forest; in 1976 this figure had risen to 7 million and the numbers continue to grow. The numbers of visitors, and their ability to penetrate many of the woodlands and the open areas, were causing damage and disturbance to wildlife, damage to grazing for commoners' stock, and major intrusion into the landscape as a result of the large numbers of cars, caravans and tents dispersed throughout the Forest, not to mention the litter left behind.

In 1970 in response to these pressures, the various parties concerned for the future of the New Forest prepared a plan which has provided the basis for management of visitors to the Forest ever since. The scheme which evolved was based both on control of access, by the creation of car-free areas controlled by locked barriers, impassable wooden posts, and ditches and banks; and the channelling of visitors to areas designated and laid out as car parks, camping or caravan sites.

'The Forest has been known and loved by a limited number of persons always; the general public have only discovered it in recent years. For one visitor twenty years ago there are scores, probably hundreds today. And year by year, as motoring becomes more common, and as cycling from being general grows, as it will, to be universal, the flow of visitors to the Forest will go on at an ever-increasing rate, and the hundreds of today will be thousands in five years' time . . .'

W H Hudson, *Hampshire Days*, 1903.

These measures have been very successfully implemented over the last fifteen years and have resolved many of the problems which were causing concern, as well as providing everything which the visitors might want. A distinctive 'house-style' has evolved as items such as car control barriers, litter bins, toilet areas, sign boards, and information points have been designed to meet specific needs. The dark timber signs, wooden gates, short timber posts and trip rails are all now a distinctive feature of the New Forest landscape. They have been extremely successful in achieving their purpose and have been sensitive to the nature of their surroundings. They have to some degree changed the character of the landscape with both desirable and, in some eyes, less desirable effects. Large areas of the Forest are now free of the intrusive effects of cars, tents and caravans leaving large areas undisturbed to be enjoyed by those venturing further afield on foot. But inevitably, simply because of the scale of provision required to cater for such large numbers of visitors, the essential trappings of a popular recreation area have to some extent had the effect of 'suburbanising' the landscape. This does not lessen the popularity of the Forest in any degree since the majority of visitors enjoy the facilities and the proximity of other people. Those who wish to escape from the visible hand of man can easily do so by walking in the remoter areas of the Forest.

The popularity of the New Forest continues unabated. But what is it about the landscape which draws so many people to it and what does their use of the Forest tell us about the way the landscape is perceived? The evidence which we can draw on to answer this question is largely circumstantial, because there has been very little investigation of what people think about the New Forest. Perhaps the major reason for its popularity is that it can easily be reached by very large numbers of people living in the surrounding towns and the conurbations of Southampton and Bournemouth. Many people will also go there out of habit, perhaps because their family has always done so, or because the Forest has been recommended by friends. A recent market research survey of trip taking in the countryside has shown such factors to be a very important influence.

As well as these general influences, the long standing tradition of free access on foot to such large areas of open heathland, grassland and woodland is undoubtedly a major attraction for those who choose to go to the Forest, especially since such freedom is so rare in the south of England. It is not simply that access is permitted. The ease with which much of the area can be reached by road, the gentle topography and the presence of many areas of short grass which provide such an easy walking surface, combine to make the New Forest a place which can be easily and conveniently enjoyed by young and old alike. While the heaths and bogs, which share some of the qualities of higher moorland, offer a challenge to the more adventurous walker, much of the landscape is gentle and welcoming, in places providing seclusion and mystery, but with none of the more forbidding qualities of some upland landscapes.

The character of the most popular parts of the Forest might be thought to give some clue as to preferences for different types of landscape; but people's choices are partly determined by where they live, and the route by which they gain access. Local residents tend to frequent the places nearest their homes, while visitors are attracted to the better known sites such as Balmer Lawn, the Rufus Stone and Hatchet Pond. Nevertheless a number of surveys have shown that the majority of people seek out sites where there are grass areas, water (either as ponds or streams) and pleasing views. There also appears to be a clear preference for edge areas, rather than for the interior of woodlands or large open spaces. The preference for grass lawns is no doubt due in part to the popularity of ball games as well as to the ease of walking which they offer and the number of ponies which they attract.

These preferences were most apparent when car access to the Forest was relatively unrestricted, before the recreation management measures were introduced. Studies carried out in 1966 identified the areas then most frequented by visitors. These included open grass areas such as Bolton's Bench, Wilverley Plain,

The New Forest is a prime example of commission policy – to cater for visitors without destroying the forest environment. Toilet blocks and camp reception offices are built from timber, as, naturally, are picnic tables, play structures and signposts.

Tony Aldous in *Tourism in Action*, 1985.

Perhaps the most controversial subject of 1976 in the New Forest was the Forestry Commission's plans for car park construction. Over the last few years there has been growing concern at the increasingly urban character of some of the recreational facilities which are being provided. The criticism has been directed more at the furniture of these sites – the notices, concrete blocks, kerbs, picnic tables and other urban paraphernalia which disfigures them – than at the location of the sites themselves.

New Forest Association, *Annual Report 1977*.

Why is the New Forest so popular? Many good reasons could be given, but above all it is the feeling of peace and freedom which makes the strongest appeal. Freedom of movement alone would today be a sufficient reason for visiting the New Forest, but add to that the visual delights – the deer, the ponies, quaint clusters of cottages sheltering amongst the mighty trees, the sea of colour that sweeps over miles of heath every autumn – and then surely there are few who can resist the Forest's invitation.

W R Myers, *The New Forest*, 1966.

The Forest provides an ideal environment for recreation — water, enclosing edges, shelter, unhindered access, pleasant views and opportunities to find both sun and shade.

The facilities for recreation are now an integral part of the landscape.

Longslade Bottom, Balmer Lawn, Stoney Cross/Ocknell Plain and Hatchet Moor, edge areas such as Aldridgehill, Hollands Wood, Burley Lawn and Denny Wood, woodland areas such as Sloden Inclosures, the Ornamental Drive, and the drive through the Knightwood Inclosure and Mark Ash Inclosure, and open heathland areas such as Deadman Hill, Picket Post, Verely Hill and Matley Heath.

The restriction of car access and limitation of camping areas means that visitor distribution is no longer quite such a clear expression of preference as it used to be. Nevertheless the car parks and camping sites provided in the conservation and management scheme generally sought to give people access to areas of similar character to those which they enjoyed previously and still offer the same variety of Forest scenery. They are located on open grass areas, the heathland, within the Ancient and Ornamental Woodlands, and on woodland edges. Some are high vantage points giving long views, some are in valleys and some are enclosed and have only woodland views. Many of the most attractive are by ponds or streams. Not surprisingly, the most heavily used still seem to coincide with the places which were originally most popular with visitors, but elsewhere use varies widely according to location. Some are favoured by local people, for example as starting points for walking the dog, while others are particularly popular with visitors. Special events, such as cricket matches, also have a marked effect on the use of individual areas.

The way that visitors use the Forest is therefore influenced by so many different factors that it does not give any very clear indication of which sorts of landscapes people particularly like, although there are some clues. It is certainly clear that visitors are very aware of the qualities of the New Forest scenery. Surveys have indicated that they particularly like the peace and quiet of the surroundings, the open space and freedom, the scenery and the animals. There is further evidence of this sensitivity to surroundings in the fact that the numbers of visitors are so sensitive to seasonal changes in the landscape, notably the flowering of the heather in late summer and the turning of the trees in autumn, both of which lead to great surges in numbers. Although there is not a great deal of interpretative material for visitors, there is a programme of guided walks to various points of interest, showing the wildlife and history of the Forest. These are very popular, indicating that visitors are indeed anxious to know more about the landscape.

Given this awareness and interest there may also be more deep rooted reasons why the New Forest is such a popular landscape. The long and complex history of the Forest and the survival intact of so much of an essentially medieval landscape is undoubtedly something which draws many visitors. It provides a sense of historical continuity which is sadly missing from much of our day to day living environment. Perhaps even more fundamental is the special relationship which we have always had with woodland. This may date from the recent past, when so much of our surroundings was wooded, and daily lives were filled with the legends, myths and mystical folklore of the forest. This image of the New Forest as a mysterious place, set apart from the rest of the world, is reinforced in the plethora of guidebooks and postcards which are available, and by the way these associations are used to promote sales of souvenirs and produce. Where else in the south of England would venison be a sought after souvenir?

For those who know little of the history or associations of the Forest, the character of the landscape itself, with its preponderance of 'edges', may be a more important factor. It is widely recognised that such 'edge' landscapes are critical in providing an attractive environment for recreation, perhaps because there is a primitive fear of being far from cover. When we wish to camp, or picnic, or simply enjoy the scenery, we instinctively seek some protection, some enclosure and some definition of space. That is why people usually choose sites at the edges of an open space, where they have partial enclosure, and this fact was deliberately used in creating the car parks and camp sites in the New Forest. Many have strong edges, defined either by gorse, or woodland. Often the edges form a gradual transition from woodland to heathland or lawn, and are easily penetrated allowing, at least psychologically, for rapid retreat to cover.

Spring, summer, autumn, winter – each season has its admirers in the Forest and therein lies the secret of its fatal charm. For it can offer pleasure to every section of the population at any time of the year. Beauty is in the eye of the beholder, bringing its own message to all who look.

Sybis Leek, *A Fool and a Tree*, 1964.

In some parts of the New Forest you sense a feeling of mystery. Perhaps this is because so much has happened there in the past that, in spite of so few traces remaining, the Forest still holds these secrets. This is particularly true of the more remote parts of the Forest to the north-west. Here small rivers wind through woods and over moorlands to the Avon valley.

Anne-Marie Edwards, *New Forest Walks*, 1982.

For hundreds of years a wealth of myth and legend has wound itself around the trees of the New Forest like a clinging vine.

O S *New Forest Leisure Guide*, 1983.

An irregular base forming bays and promontories.

From Rev. W Gilpin, Remarks on Forest Scenery, *1808 edition.*

There seems little doubt that the New Forest provides an ideal environment for informal countryside recreation. It has everything most visitors might want — water, enclosing edges, shelter, unhindered access, pleasant views and opportunities for finding both sun and shade. Landscape designers today would be hard pressed to create such a perfect environment to suit our modern tastes in outdoor leisure. The Forest might also be said, by its very nature, to have been designed for recreation. Indeed it has met the needs of leisure to varying degrees over the years since it became a Royal Forest in the eleventh century. Thus, in 1177 it was written that:

> "For the privileges of Kings are in Forests, and these are their chief delights, for they come to them to hunt when they occasionally lay aside their cares and refresh themselves with a little rest."

7. A source of artistic inspiration

The New Forest landscape has an appeal beyond the simple enjoyment of its scenery by visitors. Over the years it has proved a source of inspiration to creative artists of many types, whether painters, photographers or writers. None of the more famous writers or artists have been particularly associated with the area, but there is nevertheless a substantial collection of work inspired by the Forest, often by those with close local links. Depictions of its landscape in art and writing have influenced the image which people hold of the New Forest at the same time as the landscape itself has influenced the work of the artists and writers.

Writers and the New Forest

The original forested nature of much of our countryside perhaps explains why forests have always played an important part in English literature from the fourteenth century tales of Robin Hood, to Shakespeare's *A Midsummer Night's Dream*, to modern works such as John Fowles' *Daniel Martin*. Often they have been portrayed as separate, 'other wordly' places where mysterious events happen and, symbolically at least, the landscape belongs to all. It is these same features which writers have seized on in the New Forest.

A number of fictional works have used the Forest as a setting. The main literary association is of course *The Children of the New Forest* written by Captain Marryat in 1853. In this novel, set in the Civil War, high born children, orphaned and homeless, take to the Forest where they live as the 'lowest born' learning how to survive in the wild. The novel contains very little descriptive detail specific to the Forest but its qualities as an area wild enough and remote enough for someone to live in hiding for many years and to live from the land, are essential to the plot. In 1854 Mrs. Gaskell's famous work *North and South* first appeared. In this novel the central character Margaret Hale, moves from a luxurious life in a country

Heywood Sumner etching from J R Wise, The New Forest, *1895 edition*

42

parsonage in the New Forest, to a cotton-spinning town in the north of England. The early chapters set the scene of her background in the south as a prelude to the transition to the quite different environment of the industrial north. Trying to describe her home she says "All the other places in England that I have seen seem so hard and prosaic looking after the New Forest". She takes a pride in 'her' Forest — in the forest trees which were "all one dark, full, dusky green" in summer and bear "crimson and amber foliage" in autumn; in the ferns catching the sunlight; in the walks across the heaths; and with the picturesque scenes which she enjoys sketching.

Arthur Conan Doyle's *The White Company*, written in 1900, was also set in the Forest. The hero is brought up by the monks of Beaulieu and comes face to face with poverty, cruelty and the harshness of the Norman Forest Laws. Conan Doyle concerns himself not with the appearance of the Forest as a setting, but with the intricate detail of the social and economic conditions prevailing in the medieval forest, including the Forest Laws, the role of the keepers and verderers, the tensions between Saxon and Norman, and the medieval place-names, titles, and terminology of the time. Sir Walter Scott is another well known writer who stayed in the Forest. He is reputed to have loved its forests, moors and woods and described them in at least one poem.

Less well known than these is *Vixen* by Miss M E Braddon, a 'Forest-born girl' who "loves her native woods as Wordsworth loved his lakes and mountains". The Forest's picturesque qualities, its historical associations and its atmosphere play a large part in setting the scene, and the book describes the effect of the landscape on her personality and the way in which she observes nature closely and intimately and is restored by it. The wealth of atmosphere in the Forest, the importance of form and colour in the scene, and the memories which it holds of the past, including events such as the death of William Rufus, are all essential to the story. *Craddock Nowell* by R D Blackmore, dating from 1866, also makes much of the Forest setting but is a highly 'embroidered' novel containing many long and laboured descriptions of the landscape.

Apart from these novels much of what has been written about the New Forest landscape falls into the broad category of topographical description. Gilpin's work, already referred to, led the way in seeing the New Forest as a picturesque scene and his descriptions influenced many who came after him. Much has since been written about the 'cult of the Picturesque' in which Gilpin played such an important part. It was an aesthetic philosophy which affected various areas of the arts and has been described as "the earliest means for perceiving visual qualities in nature". Gilpin was a prolific writer and illustrator on the theme with his writings on the Wye Valley and South Wales, Cambridge and East Anglia, the Highlands of Scotland, North Wales, the Lake District and the New Forest. During his tours of these areas his specific objective was to discover which parts of the countryside of Britain best represented the 'picturesque' type of scenery. Uvedale Price and Richard Payne Knight developed the ideas, and a 'School of the Picturesque' evolved and influenced the art of landscape design as it was then practised.

In the New Forest, Gilpin's work was followed by a growth in interest in the picturesque qualities of the scenery which found expression both in descriptive writings of the nineteenth century and in art. William Cobbett, writing about the Forest in *Rural Rides* was chiefly concerned not with scenery but with practical aspects of husbandry and tree planting. He dismisses Matley Heath as "barren as it is possible for land to be" and "even worse than Bagshot Heath", but is much taken with Beaulieu and the Beaulieu River. John Wise, in his book *The New Forest: its History and Scenery* referred to the value of Gilpin's writing with its "pure love for Nature and its simple unaffected tone" but also noted how much the Forest had changed since Gilpin's time. Both Wise and Briscoe Eyre, writing a few years later, combined a

Looking West

Illustration by Heywood Sumner in The Book of Gorley, *1910.*

The sun had been getting lower and lower. There were splashes of ruddy light on the smooth grey beech boles, and that was all. Soon these would fade and all would be gloom. The grove had an awful look already. One would expect to meet some ghostly Druid or some witch of old among the shadowy tracks left by the forest wildings.

Miss M E Braddon, *Vixen*.

This leads me directly to New-foreſt, which is the ſubject of the third book. It opens with a few obſervations on this cele-brated tract of country. The ſcenery of it is next deſcribed in a ſeries of journeys through it's ſeveral diviſions;

WILLIAM GILPIN.

historical appreciation of the New Forest with unaffected descriptions of the character and qualities of the landscape they saw. Heywood Sumner, writing late in the nineteenth and in the early twentieth century continued this tradition in works such as *The Book of Gorley* and *A Guide to the New Forest*.

After Sumner, a considerable number of topographical works on the New Forest appeared, but many are notable for their flowery prose and preoccupation with local people and events rather than for their accurate description of the landscape and there is little to compare with the work of Gilpin, Wise or Sumner. More recently still, technical writings have taken over as the main source of descriptive material about the New Forest. Most are concerned with aspects of ecology, recreation, and land use history. By comparison with the earlier writers, landscape has received relatively little mention except in guides to walks and tours in the Forest.

The New Forest and the visual arts

Gilpin, as well as writing about the picturesque qualities of the New Forest, also sketched and painted what he saw. His illustrations appear in *Remarks on Forest Scenery*. As interest in picturesque scenery grew in the nineteenth century, the New Forest became extremely popular as a landscape to paint. This popularity culminated with a special exhibition in London in 1875, shortly before the House of Commons Select Committee met to consider the future of the Forest. The exhibition was intended to help the nation to form a proper assessment of the value of what was then considered to be a unique area, by bringing together "pictures, drawings and studies of its varied and characteristic scenery".

Nearly 250 pictures were gathered together for this exhibition which was held to have been extremely well attended. None of the more well known artists of the time appear to have been involved, although in 1820 John Constable had painted 'Cottages and Trees in the New Forest'. Two petitions presented to the select committee at the time, one by artists, and one by people engaged in literary and professional work, were signed by some of the great names of the time. They argued that the New Forest represented "one of the best possible schools of art that the nation could possess" and pleaded for "preservation at home of important sketching grounds". William Shayer and Walter Crane were among the better known artists who represented scenes from the New Forest in this period. Crane's first commission was to prepare the illustrations for Wise's book.

The growth of artistic interest in the New Forest at this time was caused by many factors including the interest in nature and the picturesque, the ease of access by the new railway and the growing desire to escape from increasingly industrialised surroundings. Threats to the Forest, and particularly to the 'natural scenery' and the sense that this was a resource which belonged to everyone, also had their effect and, more practically, it seems that the artists also found a ready market for their work.

After 1875, interest in the New Forest as a source of artistic inspiration continued with the work of Heywood Sumner, and Frederick Golden Short, both of whom lived in the Forest. Sumner's etchings appeared in the Artist's edition of Wise's book in 1885 and he also illustrated his own writings, using a rather different representational style. The work of these and many of the earlier artists was displayed in a more recent exhibition in Christchurch under the title *Painters of the New Forest 1800-1920*. Today, although other forms of visual art have assumed greater importance, the tradition is continued in the work of local artist Barry Peckham, whose subject matter is drawn primarily from the Forest and includes individual tree studies, woodland and heathland scenes and, increasingly, New Forest ponies. His work has been exhibited at the Royal Academy.

From the high ground the hills of the Isle of Wight rise in the south east and on every side the forest falls in fold beyond fold of green and purple and gold. In the early spring there are more shades of green than ever an artist could imagine possible – the green of roadside lawns, the green of bogs, of gorse, of beech and of oak, or pine and of larch, of aspen and of silver birch. In the autumn the colours defy reproduction. I have never seen a painting however wild and impossible which reached the full measure of the glory.

Ralph Wightman, *The Wessex Heathland*, 1953.

It is a well-known fact that not a few English artists of note considered the New Forest as their favourite resort for study and recreation, and also from abroad a number of painters of forest landscape are attracted every year by its unique scenery.

New Forest Exhibition Catalogue, 1875

I did not half appreciate the New Forest until I had travelled, but I do not hesitate to say now, that there is nothing like it anywhere else in the world, taking the forest in its natural state; that such is the opinion of most travellers, British and Foreign, and also the opinion of British and Foreign Artists.

G E Briscoe Eyre, in Evidence to 1875 Select Committee.

View of Frame Wood, Brockenhurst.

Walter Crane illustration from J R Wise, The New Forest, *1895 edition.*

Through the last two centuries the same themes have recurred in paintings of the Forest. They include many studies of the natural forms, light, colour, shade and incident which are so much a part of the picturesque landscape; studies attempting to capture the essential spirit of the Forest; close studies of particular landmarks (eg 'The Queen's Bower' by Heywood Sumner), representations of historical or romantic association (eg 'The Rufus Glade' by Lancelot Speed and 'The Red King' by Hartley Desmond) and numerous studies of animals and traditional activities (eg 'Colt Hunting in the New Forest' by Lucy Kemp Welch and 'Staghunt' by John Emms).

Painters often create the popular imagery of an area — for example Constable's Suffolk and Crome's Norfolk. To some extent, this has happened for the New Forest with the work of painters such as Shayer and Golden Short. They were not nationally well known figures but they have helped to shape the way that others have seen the Forest.

Another form of visual art is currently influencing the popular image of the New Forest, namely photography. Most visitors are influenced not only by what they see for themselves, but by the images in guidebooks and in postcards. Today the photographs of Richard Kraus are providing striking and widely available images of the Forest. These photographs, a selection of which appeared in the book *An English Forest* and a number of which are now reproduced as postcards, table mats and offprints, represent a particular aspect of the New Forest landscape. They are all taken at dawn and concentrate upon the effects of light and mist on tree forms, woodland and heathland. The open landscape of the Forest makes it a popular setting for films, television and advertisements. The current interest in wildlife photography makes the New Forest of particular interest and the work of Eric Ashby, who lives in the Forest, and of Simon King, has been notable. Many of these films build on the image of the New Forest as an old landscape, rich in history and with a wealth of wildlife hidden away in this very special and 'separate' place.

In both the visual and literary arts, inspiration comes from these special attributes of the New Forest — from its separate, 'other worldliness', its mystery, the myth and legend which surrounds it and the unique way of life which it supports. All this serves to build and reinforce a very strong sense of place.

. . . it gives, more than any other place, a far greater range of subject, in sea, and moor, and valley; because too, the traveller can here go where he pleases without any of those lets and hindrances which take away so much pleasure; and, lastly, because here can best be seen Nature's crown of glory – her woods.

J R Wise, The New Forest : Its History and Scenery, First Edition, 1863.

There is no doubt whatever that this forest has a poetical original beauty which is without a rival not only in these islands but also on the Continent, and the artist may well be pardoned if on this subject he has perhaps a stronger feeling than even the politician and sanitarian.

New Forest Exhibition Catologue, 1875.

Latchmore shade.

Illustration by Heywood Sumner in A Guide to the New Forest, *1925 edition.*

8. The importance of the New Forest landscape

It has as long been recognised that the New Forest is an outstandingly important landscape. Over a hundred years ago, in evidence to the House of Commons Select Committee, a Mr Lovell let the Committee know exactly how strongly he felt about its qualities and about the need to protect it for the future when he said:

> "The New Forest, as a whole, is one of the most beautiful Districts remaining in this country, and indeed the only one of its kind in England. This is owing to its varied character, and to the intermingling of open heaths, undulating ground, and odd woods, scattered over it in all parts. Unless it is preserved in its integrity and unity, as a whole, it will be destroyed as an object of great national value, an object of value as great as exists in any work of art, although the New Forest is one of nature".

Today its unique qualities continue to give the New Forest an outstanding place in our national heritage.

Why is the New Forest landscape so important?

It must be emphasised first of all that the New Forest is widely recognised as being of great national and international importance because of its existing ecology and the historical evolution of the ecology under the influence of grazing, common rights and woodland management over a period of over 900 years. From this standpoint it is widely agreed to be one of the most important areas of 'natural' vegetation in Europe. The remainder of this chapter should be read with this in mind, since the fact that it deals with landscape should not be seen as underplaying the ecological perspective — the two are in fact complementary.

Returning to consideration of the New Forest as an area of outstanding landscape, rather than an extremely valuable complex of ecological habitats, why is it that it should be considered such an important place? There are four reasons:

An historical landscape

First and foremost, is the value of the New Forest as an historical landscape. It is the most intact survival of a medieval hunting forest and, though the landscape is now much changed, there are still very clear links with the past. From the archaeological viewpoint the potential of the whole area for providing as yet undiscovered evidence about the nature of settlement and land use in the pre-Norman period gives considerable weight to its value as an historical landscape. Furthermore, of all the former Royal Forests, only the New Forest survives in anything like its medieval form as an institution. The influence of centuries of management can still be seen in the modern landscape and the changes which are taking place now continue to reflect both the historical influences which still prevail today (with commoning and woodland management foremost among them) as well as some of the newer ones, such as the rapid growth of recreation. It is not only that the landscape itself is a living reminder of the long history of the Forest, but also that there is such a wealth of documentary material available which allows almost every aspect of its evolution to be examined in detail. This gives the landscape added meaning. Last, but not least, the historical importance of the Forest is enhanced by its strong associations with important historical figures, notably William Rufus.

A unique landscape type

As a result of its history, and the ecological pattern which has developed in response to it and is itself of such high value, the New Forest is also unique as a particular type of landscape. Nowhere else in Britain today is it possible to find such a combination, or such an extent of matured deciduous woodland, inclosure woodland, open heathland and grass lawns, disposed together to form such a complex and attractive

Heywood Sumner etching from J R Wise, The New Forest, *1895 edition*

. . . an historic forest which, though at our very doors, is unique in Europe, – unique in its primitive condition, unique in its extent, variety, and beauty, unique in its power to inspire, instruct, and improve the artist, and to afford in its calm sequestered solitudes that repose which the ever-increasing whirl of business and professional life renders yearly more and more indispensable to all classes of society.

New Forest Exhibition Catalogue, 1875.

On the right, and at no great distance are thick woods of the finest timber in England and even on the crest of the hill, a fine rounded wood of beech and oak, Matley Wood stands up like a fertile island, with a sea of heather and bog around it. To the left lies the great stretch of Matley Bog . . . Here is a picture which, but for the road and bridge, cannot have changed for a thousand years. A stream flows down from a wide valley in the thick woods, and spreads itself among green marshes, sedge and alder copses, at the top of the bog, whose level and impassable plain loses itself in the black heath which stretches far beyond the railway into the southern forest.

C J Cornish, The New Forest, *1910.*

. . . it would be pity if the lawns were completely lost, for they provide a most attractive foil to the eternal background of forest trees and a refreshing change from the wilder and barren heaths.

W R Myers, The New Forest, *1966.*

mosaic, with the added bonus of numerous grazing animals and a wealth of flora and fauna. Although this sort of combination was once typical of other Royal Forests, few examples of any size remain elsewhere in the country.

Nowhere else in lowland Britain is there such an extent of heathland as remains in the New Forest. Although heathland of similar character occurs in areas such as the Ashdown Forest and some of the Surrey heaths, it is on a much smaller scale and more fragmented in its occurrence. In the whole of Europe comparable types, of what is known as Anglo-Norman heath, have also declined markedly over the years — to such an extent that the New Forest now represents approximately half of the total area which remains. It is the most important tract of such vegetation in Europe, and its conservation is of international significance.

The Ancient and Ornamental Woodlands are unique. There is no area in Britain or indeed in north west Europe with such an extent of old woodland, with so many old trees, or demonstrating the same lack of significant intervention over such a long period. While there are remnants of such woods, and of other original components of Royal Forests, in places such as Epping Forest, Hatfield Forest, Sherwood Forest, Hainault Forest, Savernake Forest and the Forest of Dean, nowhere else do they remain on such an extensive scale or in such a characteristic combination as in the New Forest. Nor, in general, are they accompanied by survival of the original medieval form of administration.

A landscape with aesthetic appeal

This unique landscape is also aesthetically appealing to a wide range of people. Over the years it has inspired writers, artists and photographers whose work has helped to shape other people's image of the Forest and the scenery is now enjoyed by many millions of people each year. But why is it that the New Forest has this appeal?

Theories abound as to why we have preferences for certain types of landscape and, while none have been 'proved' to be correct, it is perhaps significant to find that all of them can help to explain the universally strong appeal of the New Forest.

Some argue that the appeal of certain types of landscape is purely a matter of taste, which changes with time and with fashion. English landscape taste has been described as favouring, among other qualities, the bucolic (ie the rural or pastoral), the picturesque, the deciduous and the antique. The New Forest certainly demonstrates all of these qualities and should therefore appeal to those who share such particularly 'English' tastes. The picturesque qualities of the landscape, which so attracted Gilpin's attention, may have a particular significance since we all tend to have an image of ideal countryside which has been influenced by the work of painters and also by those who designed the great eighteenth and nineteenth century landscape parks.

Other theories say that our preferences have biological evolutionary roots, going back to the days when our ancestors had to fight to survive in a hostile world. They would argue that we prefer some landscapes because they have characteristics which distant memories, of instincts long since buried by our surface civilisation, tell us are helpful to our survival. One such theory argues that landscapes are distinguished by the extent to which they offer 'prospect', that is long views from high places or over flat open ground, or 'refuge', that is enclosed, sheltered and secure hiding places. Both prospect and refuge are considered important for survival, providing the opportunity, in some circumstances, to see without being seen. The New Forest is a landscape which, with its unique combination of extensive open heathland interspersed with dense woodland and an abundance of 'edges', provides a balance of both prospect and refuge which we may, intuitively, find most appealing.

The main feature of the Northern area is open moorland – level, upland plains, capped with gravel, covered with heather, furze and bracken, worn into five parallel ridges and bottoms by streams that trickle in dry, and rush in wet weather down to the Avon. Here and there the hills are overgrown with thickets, with old woods, with planted Inclosures, or with self-sown Scots pine, but the open Forest is never far distant.

Heywood Sumner, *A Guide to the New Forest*, 1925.

Standing as it does in its primitive state, it presents opportunities for the study of nature in perhaps her grandest and most picturesque forms. The elegance and stateliness of its trees – beech, birch, and oak – the lovely undergrowth, infinite in variety of line and tint, and the sombre, I had almost said the solemn tone which characterises it, makes this forest singularly improvising and instructive to the artist.

New Forest Exhibition Catalogue, 1875.

I find that, in the opinion of artists, its value is beyond calculation. Both British and Foreign artists say that there is nothing like it anywhere else. They say that it is particularly valuable for its suggestiveness, or, as artists say, its power of inspiration, and also, indeed, for its power of instruction to young artists.

G E Briscoe Eyre, in Evidence to 1875 Select Committee.

In this "prospect" of the forest the eye sees nothing but woods, commons, and heaths, not in squares and patches, but in a succession of long ridges which seem to run out from right to left from a shoulder of higher land to the west.

C J Cornish, *The New Forest*, 1910.

Mystery, where a landscape promises more information than is actually revealed, and symbolism, are also believed by some to play an important part in landscape preferences. The old woodlands of the New Forest offer both in profusion with their long history, and medieval associations. There seems little doubt that we have special feelings about such landscapes. We can measure ourselves against old trees, both physically, and in terms of age. Furthermore these woodlands are among the few remaining examples of traditional wood pasture (a term used for any type of land on which the growing of trees is combined with the grazing of stock) which, as Richard Mabey points out in his book *The Common Ground*, is "a close approximation to our image of an ancient forest". He goes on to point out that such landscapes provide:

> "an image of one of our basic ancestral habitats . . . that bears the unmistakeable handprint of a long relationship between man and nature. Townspeople enjoying these landscapes are, in a sense, just returning home".

This special relationship with such a woodland environment is an often repeated theme even in popular guides read by today's visitors. In the Ordnance Survey's *Leisure Guide* we find similar sentiments:

> "Today, the Forest exercises a powerful hold on our imagination, rekindling images of a once-pastoral Britain clothed with copse, thicket and close. We come because we have, as a people, a deep, almost umbilical, relationship with woodland".

An outstanding landscape for recreation

Whatever the underlying reasons for its popularity, the New Forest is of outstanding importance as a landscape for recreation. Apart from its intrinsic appeal, and its accessibility, this is primarily because of the opportunities it offers for unhindered access on foot to open land and the excellent provision which has been made for its enjoyment. Although there is no absolute legal right of access, there has long been an accepted privilege to enjoy 'air and exercise' on the Crown Land. In effect this gives free access to wander over 47,073 acres of open forest.

This represents more extensive free access than in many of the national parks. In fact it is worth noting that the New Forest is perhaps the nearest thing in England and Wales to a true national park. In a widely used classification system for protected areas devised by the International Union for the Conservation of Nature and Natural Resources (IUCN), national parks are the most protected category. They are tracts of natural or semi-natural landscape not generally altered by human exploitation or habitation, with features of special interest, where visitors are allowed to enter for recreation. They are usually owned or controlled by the State. By contrast the national parks of England and Wales are settled, and exploited and are largely privately owned with access limited accordingly. They fall within IUCN Category 5 'protected landscapes' rather than being true national parks. The New Forest with its considerable extent of Crown land managed by the State, with special provision for conservation, and with freedom for visitors to wander at will on foot, is much closer to the international model of a national park.

The value of the landscape for recreation is reflected in the number of visitors to the New Forest. In 1985 it was estimated that there were some 9 million visitors in a year, together with approximately a further 600,000 people who came to camp overnight. This total figure of over 9.5 million visitors to an area of only 145 square miles, means that, per square mile, the New Forest received more visitors than even the Peak District National Park which is the most visited of the national parks.

Take a road that enters, from an open space, the gloom and shadow of the wood. There is a purple – a dark and yet a colour-filled – mystery about as it dives out of the sunlight into the gloom, that gives promise of all sorts of delightful fairy-lands and secrets within.

Horace G Hutchinson, *The New Forest*, 1904 (& 1906).

The warm glow of sunset streams along hill and slope, illumining at times some group of beech till the very boughs and limbs grow indistinct radiant with lambent flame, or paints a background to the towering grove; and level rays of autumn search the inmost recesses of the forest.

G E Briscoe Eyre, 'The New Forest' A sketch from *The Fortnightly Review*, April 1st 1871.

There is nowhere else like the New Forest in the world. By some miracle, the oldest and largest medieval Forest in Europe has survived here, in the crowded south of England, just over one hour's train ride from London. And, even more surprising, most of its glorious wilderness is very little known. A few minutes walk from the noisy centres or one of the many car parks sited along the roads, and the real New Forest is waiting for you to discover it. Silent, delightful and with an incredible richness of scenery and wildlife; you will find it a magical forest.

Anne-Marie Edwards, *The Unknown Forest* A walkers guide, 1981.

Recognition of the quality of the New Forest landscape

These different values, which together make the New Forest such a special place, are by no means a recent discovery. The quality of the New Forest landscape has been recognised by many people over the last two centuries since Gilpin first extolled its virtues.

Such recognition has often been couched in terms of its merits as a 'national park'. For example in 1875, before the Select Committee Inquiry, Henry Fawcett, then Professor of Political Economy at Cambridge University, referred to the Forest as a 'national park' of greater value to the nation than any picture, gallery or museum. Just over fifty years later, in 1930, Vaughan Cornish in *National Parks and the Heritage of Scenery* described it as "already in effect a National Park" and gave evidence to this effect, to the National Parks Committee.

In 1945, the New Forest was recommended by John Dower as a conservation area in his report on national parks in England and Wales. Dower noted that he would have proposed it as a national park if he had not been satisfied that in future it would be adequately dealt with by the Forestry Commission. In the subsequent 1947 report of the National Parks Committee the New Forest was included among the conservation areas to be designated on account of their high landscape quality, scientific interest and recreational value.

Its special status as Crown Land and the special arrangements for its administration have in fact always made it an exception to the general policy of formal designation for outstanding areas of countryside in England and Wales. For this reason it was eventually excluded from the area designated as the South Hampshire Coast Area of Outstanding Natural Beauty.

At present, the value of the New Forest is recognised in a number of ways. The Ministerial Mandate emphasises its importance as 'national heritage'; its designation as a site of special scientific interest recognises its high ecological value; both the South West Hampshire Structure Plan and the Forest and Downlands Villages Local Plan contain policies and statements which recognise the value of the New Forest landscape. The development by the New Forest District Council of the concept of a New Forest Heritage Area gives further recognition to its importance and attempts to establish the interrelationships between the Forest itself and adjacent areas of countryside.

The Countryside Commission considers that the New Forest is of equivalent quality to a national park for the natural beauty and amenity of its landscape and the opportunities it affords for open air recreation. It believes that the Forest should be considered on a par with the best of Britain's scenery, ranking, despite its very different character, alongside such areas as the Lake District, Snowdonia, the Yorkshire Dales and Dartmoor. Equally it believes that landscape conservation and appropriate provision for informal recreation should be pursued with the same vigour as in the national parks and that the necessary resources are made available for it.

Conclusion

In summary then, the New Forest is of outstanding importance as a unique historical landscape, as a unique type of landscape combining elements which are themselves increasingly rare and which are found nowhere else in Britain on the same scale, as a landscape which has a considerable degree of aesthetic appeal both to the general public and to writers, artists and photographers who have found inspiration there, and as a landscape ideally suited to countryside recreation. The features which appear to contribute most to its value are the Ancient and Ornamental Woodlands, the older deciduous plantations, the open lawns, especially where they are of an intimate scale combined with attractive woodland edges, the Forest streams and water bodies, the wilder areas of open heathland, and the contrasting landscapes of the Beaulieu River and the Solent foreshore.

The traditional character of the Forest depends on its unique wildlife, on the special qualities of the landscape, and on the way in which both are continuing to evolve in response to the demands made by those who live and work in the area, or visit it for recreation. The New Forest landscape speaks to us with many voices. As Gilpin wrote:

"The forest, like other beautiful scenes, pleases the eye, but its great effect is to rouse the imagination".

Palmers Slough

Illustration by Heywood Sumner in The Book of Gorley, *1910.*

Appendices

1. Some facts and figures about the New Forest

Location and extent

The New Forest is in south west Hampshire between Southampton and Bournemouth. The present perambulation covers an area of 145 square miles (375 square kilometeres) or 92,734 acres (37,544 hectares).

Planning designations covering the New Forest

Green Belt designation covers almost the whole perambulation. Within this designated area construction of new buildings and change of use of existing buildings will not normally be permitted for purposes other than agriculture, forestry and development to replace existing dwellings which have been continuously occupied.

South Hampshire Coast Area of Outstanding Natural Beauty covers the part of the perambulation covered by the Beaulieu Estate and adjacent enclosed land, the Beaulieu River and the Solent Foreshore.

New Forest Heritage Area designated by the New Forest District Council, including an area of peripheral land outside the perambulation. It is intended to ensure continuity of ecological habitats, to avoid development in adjacent areas having an adverse effect on the Forest, and to protect a pool of marginal agricultural land which is used as grazing land in conjuction with New Forest Grazing.

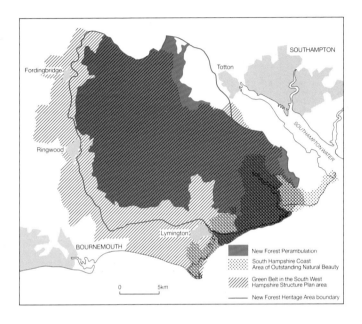

Status of land

Category	Areas	
	Hectares	Acres
Private commons, agricultural and residential land	10,522	25,999
Open Forest (Crown Land)	18,376	45,407
Total enclosable land Including:	8,646	21,364
Inclosures under 1877 Act	(7,141)	(17,645)
Inclosures under 1949/64 Acts	(813)	(2,010)
Crown freehold inclosures	(494)	(1,220)
Leasehold land	(198)	(489)
Total	37,544	92,770

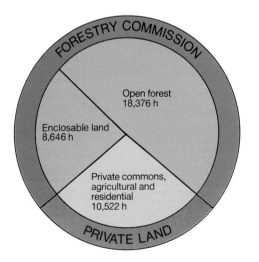

Types of woodland in inclosures

| Type | Areas | |
	Hectares	Acres
Coniferous high forest	4,744	11,723
Including: Scots pine	(1,692)	(4,181)
Douglas Fir	(1,021)	(2,522)
Corsican pine	(1,102)	(2,724)
Larch	(238)	(588)
Spruce	(534)	(1,319)
Other	(157)	(389)
Conifer/Broadleaved mixture	891	2,202
Broadleaved high forest	2,744	6,781
Including: Pure oak	(1,384)	(3,420)
Oak/beech	(942)	(2,328)
Beech	(299)	(739)
Other	(119)	(294)

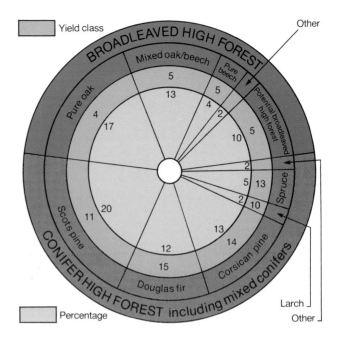

Types of vegetation within Open Forest

| Types of vegetation | Areas (Approximate) | |
	Hectares	Acres
Ancient and Ornamental Broadleaved Woodland	3,381	8,351
Self-sown pine woodland*	211	521
Calluna heathland	5,913	14,605
Valley bogs and wet heath	2,835	7,002
Agrostis/Molinia grassland with bracken and gorse	5,712	14,114
Forest lawns	324	800

(*Note: A further 1,176 acres (477 hectares) of self-sown pine occur on the Open Forest but are scheduled for clearance.)

Recreation in the New Forest

Number of car parks, excluding adjacent commons	141
Number of car parking spaces, including adjacent commons	5,303
Capacity of camp sites (pitches)	4,870
Extent of car free areas	18,300 hectares
Extent of car parks and camp sites	242 hectares
Estimated total visitors per annum	10 million
Camper nights per annum	750,000
Estimated day visits per annum	9.25 million

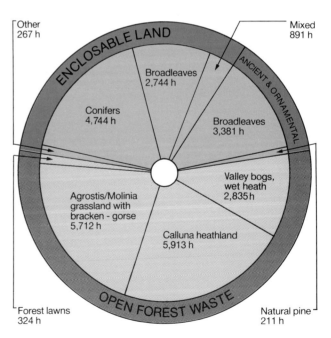

2. Summary of main provisions of New Forest Acts

1698 Enclosure Act (9 & 10. William III. Ch. 36)
Recognised rights of common and provided for enclosure and planting of 2,000 acres, plus 200 acres annually for 20 years.

1808 Enclosure Act (48. George III. Ch. 19)
Provided for enclosure up to a total of 6,000 acres at one time.

1851 Deer Removal Act (16 & 17. Victoria. Ch. 19)
Deer should be removed.
Crown took powers of enclosure of 10,000 acres in addition to that already permitted.
Established a 'rolling power' of enclosure.

1877 New Forest Act (40 & 41. Victoria. Ch. 121)
Restrict the right of the Crown to enclose to a maximum of 16,000 acres at any time.
Removed restrictions on common grazing.
Constituted Court of Verderers.

1949 New Forest Act (12 & 13. George VI. Ch. 69)
Reconstituted Verderers and extended their powers.
Forestry Commission (FC) made responsible for controlling coarse herbage, scrub and trees on the Open Forest.
FC given further powers to enclose, with consent of Verderers up to 5,000 more acres of Open Forest.
FC given powers to enclose areas up to 20 acres in Ancient and Ornamental Woods, to help regeneration.
FC given duty to prepare atlas of holdings with common rights.
Powers taken to fence main A31 trunk road to reduce accidents with animals.

1964 New Forest Act (12 & 13. Elizabeth II. Ch. 83)
Extended perambulation to include adjacent commons, making them subject to Verderer's Bye Laws.
Required Verderer's and Forestry Commission to have regard to desirability of conserving flora, fauna and geological and physiographical features.
Powers for the gridding and fencing of A35 and erection of drift fences.
Gave Verderers powers to control means of access to Forest and to prevent interference with fences without their consent.

1970 New Forest Act (18 & 19. Elizabeth II. Ch. 21)
FC given powers to enclose land, with agreement of Verderers, for purposes of providing facilities for recreation. Powers for fencing A337 Cadnam to Lymington Road.

3. Useful references

Countryside Commission, *The New Forest Commoners*, CCP 164, 1984.

G E B Eyre, 'The New Forest: A Sketch', *Fortnightly Review*, 1st April, 433-451, 1871.

Forestry Commission, *New Forest Management Plan 1982-91*, 1982.

Forestry Commission, *Explore the New Forest*, HMSO, 1975.

Forestry Commission, A *Review of Treatment of Scots Pine Stands made in 1977*, 1977.

W Gilpin, *Remarks on Forest Scenery and other Woodland views*, relative chiefly to picturesque beauty, illustrated by the scenery of the New Forest, Hampshire, T Cadell and W Davies, 1791.

Nature Conservancy Council, *The New Forest, Hampshire, Management Proposals for the Unenclosed Woodlands and Woodlands of Special Importance in the Statutory Inclosures*, 1982.

New Forest Working Party, *Conservation of the New Forest*, 1970.

New Forest Commoner's Defence Association, A *Survey of Scots Pine on the Open Waste of the New Forest*, 1973.

New Forest Technical Review Group, *Progress Report on the Implementation of Conservation Measures 1972-76 and Proposals for Future Strategy*, 1976.

Ordnance Survey/Automobile Association, Leisure Guide: *New Forest*, 1983.

H Sumner, *The Book of Gorley*, H M Gilbert, 1910.

H Sumner, *A Guide to the New Forest*, 1924.

C R Tubbs, *The New Forest, An Ecological History*, David and Charles, 1968.

J R Wise, *The New Forest: Its History and Scenery*, Smith Elder, 1863.

More comprehensive references are given in a bibliography prepared by Nicholas Flower and published by the Nature Conservancy Council as No. 3 in their Bibliography Series.